GOOD NEWS
IS BAD NEWS
IS GOOD NEWS

To Jim & Gail

GOOD NEWS
IS BAD NEWS
IS GOOD NEWS

William K. McElvaney

ORBIS BOOKS
Maryknoll, New York 10545

Saint Paul School of Theology, Kansas City, Missouri, will receive all royalties from the sale of *Good News Is Bad News Is Good News.*

Second Printing, June 1980

The Catholic Foreign Mission Society of America (Maryknoll) recruits and trains people for overseas missionary service. Through Orbis Books Maryknoll aims to foster the international dialogue that is essential to mission. The books published, however, reflect the opinions of their authors and are not meant to represent the official position of the society.

Library of Congress Cataloging in Publication Data

McElvaney, William K.   1928-
  Good news is bad news is good news.

  Includes bibliographical references.
  1. Liberation theology.   I. Title.
BT83.57.M23   261.8   79-22032
ISBN 0-88344-157-8

Contents

PART TWO
LIBERATION THEOLOGY FOR PRIVILEGED AND PROSPEROUS CHRISTIANS

Preface

José Míguez Bonino is one of the presidents of the World Council of Churches. He is also an evangelical "liberation theologian" who teaches at an ecumenical seminary in Buenos Aires. I have visited him twice in the past three years at ISEDET (the Buenos Aires seminary). Each time we have met he has talked about the "verticality of revolution," arguing that the primary hope for genuine liberation in Latin America resides in the radical transformation of values, institutions, loyalties, and lifestyles in the United States. The impact of U.S. policies, systems, and values on Latin America cannot be overstated. Míguez insists that unless something happens to *us* (in North America) the future is bleak "south of the border."

In November 1978, I met with a group of church leaders in Argentina. We were talking about Billy Graham and Oral Roberts, about electronic television and the present emphasis on "evangelism" in my country. Referring to the revival many are praying for in the United States, these South American sisters and brothers suggested that unless our consumer-oriented, materialistic values are converted, and unless our lifestyles and political action truly reflect that conversion, our "salvation" will be a cultural phenomenon that has little bearing on the outcome of the struggle of the world's poor, dehumanized, and dispossessed—and only a remote relationship to the Gospel of Jesus Christ.

It is for these very reasons that *Good News Is Bad News Is Good News* is an extremely important book. The book market in the United States is glutted with manuscripts written by white males for middle-class consumption. This book is no exception—yet it is a marvelous exception. Written by a white male and directed toward "privileged and prosperous Christians," it explores the claims and authority of liberation theology. While learning from and interpreting Latin American theologians, the author turns his primary attention toward racism, sexism, and glittering consumerism in the U.S.A. Pleading for Christian involvement in a world of poverty and pain he writes, "Exposing oneself to liberation theology is obviously not a form of armchair recreation." The following pages will provide little relaxation, little peace of mind. Rather, they will provide an arena for hemispheric discussion, a disturbing context for probing the classism, racism, and sexism endemic to our immediate culture and a mirror in which we can see ourselves as others see us.

Two of McElvaney's prime strengths in helping build bridges between the harsh and angry rhetoric of many liberation theologians and the self-serving lethargy of many middle-class Christians are his incisive, penetrating, and faithful use of the Bible and his obvious pastoral concern. He does not launch a diatribe against the middle class; he speaks from within it and acknowledges his complicity with it. He writes, "It is the story of God's free grace that is also always God's costly grace, a grace that saves us by sending us into the world for God, for others, and when all is said and done, for our own salvation."

Some years ago in introducing a slim volume titled *Mission: Middle America* (Abingdon, 1971), I said, "There are qualities of true greatness in Middle America. I am profoundly thankful for my beginnings in its soil and my present relationship to it. I pray that those of us who are a part of it may be open to the will of God as he tries to lead us into ways of radical change and essential new life." With this volume Bill McElvaney has helped me better understand those words and has helped answer that prayer.

James Armstrong, Resident Bishop,
The United Methodist Church, Dakotas Area

Introduction

If I were a pastor in the church today, as I was for fifteen years, I would be looking for ways to come to grips with liberation theology in relation to the local congregation. If I were a layperson struggling to be alive to the pertinent issues confronting Christianity today, I most likely would be looking for help in relating my faith and that of the church to Third World, ethnic, and feminist concerns. Were I a seminarian expecting graduation into a parish, I'd be wanting to translate my seminary knowledge of liberation theologies into a faithful and effective ministry. *Good News Is Bad News Is Good News* is an attempt to translate Third World, ethnic, and feminist theologies into the idiom of a Fourth Liberation Theology— for the privileged and prosperous Christian community.

Liberation is a dominant theme in Christian theology today. I hope it will continue to be. Liberation theology from the Third World emerges from the cauldron of hunger, deprivation, and powerlessness, conditions which describe the misery of the majority. Black theology, as well as other expressions of ethnic theologies, focuses on past and present patterns of white racism in the United States. Liberation theology from a feminist perspective profoundly probes the ancient and traditional sexist patterns in church and culture. These theologies tend to have similar methodologies, and in spite of marked differences, all are especially concerned to theologize with basic variables of the people's experience in mind: suffering, dehumanization, and marginal existence.

All the books that I've read on liberation theology understandably center on liberation for the outcast, the exploited, the poor. However, from a biblical standpoint God's liberating love is offered to all, including the privileged and the prosperous of the world. I have come to believe that the changes envisioned by liberation theologies are not guilt-inducing imperatives which bring despair or paralysis, but rather the liberating claim and consequence of God's unconditional and unbounded love for us all. In essence this book is about the God who loves us enough to disturb us, whose Good News is often Bad News from the standpoint of our present point of reference . . . and inevitably Good News when our life posture and priorities become those of the liberating Word. As the late Martin Luther King, Jr., used to say, we are talking about "the soul of America." To disregard the suffering and exploitation of others dehumanizes not only those who suffer, but also those who are privileged and prosperous.

The style of this book is intended to be pastoral and personal rather than polemical. Embedded in almost every page is my own journey into the promises and claims of the Christian Gospel. Where these probings are leading me I cannot know in advance, but I am sure that God is introducing me to a more profound experience and realization of the disturbing yet saving love of Jesus Christ. Indeed, this work is more a personal pilgrimage in process than a technical treatise on either a theological system or the complexities of Christian social involvement. Nevertheless, there is theological reflection as it relates to lifestyles and systems. To say this another way, attitudes and basic presuppositions will receive more attention than theories of power.

Much of this material is a mixture of insights from various liberation theologians with my own reflections and experiences. Liberation theologians help us to see ourselves as others see us, constituting more often than not vehicles of God's disturbing love. The experiential factor identifies my situation with most of those for whom this book is intended. I readily concede that a white male has to be a fool even to attempt a hearing and then an application of feminist, ethnic, and Third World theologies, especially under one cover. But to be that kind of fool is exactly what the God of liberation is asking of privileged and prosperous Christians in this hour of history. At least if one is to be a fool, be it for first-rate things!

In using the term "the privileged and the prosperous," I'm inviting you to think in global terms. If you drive a car, pay income tax, have a decent roof over your head, eat as regularly as you choose, have any savings, own anything, travel occasionally, enjoy some leisure time free from want, or any combination of these, you belong somewhere on the scale of the privileged and prosperous in relation to the misery of the earth's majority. If in addition you are a white male, as I am, you in all likelihood enjoy the additional "privilege" of not having to experience the oppression of racism and sexism.

Although liberation has to do with identifying with those who hurt, I am under no illusion that massive numbers of the privileged and the prosperous will willingly respond to the revamping of systems of power, affluence, and influence. Neither am I under the equally naive illusion that

God is powerless to bring about new possibilities in history, either individually or collectively. Even with a well-informed understanding of the limits of the human condition, none of us can arbitrarily rule out what the activating love of God may bring about tomorrow in your life, my life, or in our common life together. I believe there are considerable numbers of Christians today, both clergy and laity, who are either already struggling with these issues or who could do so with some help within the Christian community.

In using quotes that include sexist language I have not changed the original, although in my own use of language I seek to be inclusive. The importance of this issue is discussed in Chapter Seven. The writings of several liberation theologians have pushed me along the way in this project. Particularly helpful have been James Cone, Rosemary Ruether, Letty Russell, Gustavo Gutiérrez, and José Míguez Bonino. I am thankful to the Texas Conference of Churches, to a number of Annual Conferences of the United Methodist Church, and to United States Army Chaplains in Europe for the opportunity to explore some of these themes in lectures and sermons and for the encouraging reception which buoyed my efforts. I am greatly indebted to the following readers for their critique of various portions of the manuscript: Wilfred M. Bailey, Victor P. Furnish, Llewellyn M. Heigham, Jean C. Lambert, James M. Lawson, Jr., Tex S. Sample, Susan S. Vogel, and James F. White. The diversity of perspectives offered by these readers was both enlightening and significant for many improvements, although the remaining shortcomings belong to me alone.

The supportive and challenging context of the Saint Paul School of Theology community has been an indispensable factor in making possible the writing task. I owe a special gratitude to Ruth Grinager, Diane McGrew, Joyce White, Natalie Keirn, and Jo Lafler for the long, difficult endeavor of manuscript typing and assembling. The final manuscript was typed by Norma Damon. To each of these persons I say, "Thank you for making this manuscript possible."

PART ONE

Listening to Liberation Theologies

CHAPTER ONE

Out of Oppression and into Restored Community

In the early 1960s I was the originating pastor of a new congregation on the east side of Dallas. After many months of preparation we launched a building program with plans for a unique free-form edifice composed of concrete blocks and a bonding material called "archilithics." During the construction process and even at completion, the comments of observers ranged from A to Z. "Looks like a sewage disposal plant." "The most intriguing building I've ever seen." "An eyesore and a disgrace to the neighborhood." "A remarkable and courageous blend of the ancient with the contemporary." To me the most memorable comment was from the person who said, "You may be offended by it, or you may think it's the greatest. But there is one thing you cannot do in relation to this building. You cannot ignore it."[1]

Liberation theologies cannot be ignored by the Christian community. For some the thrust of these theologies represents the most encouraging sign in years from the Christian church. For others liberation theologies are at best passing fads of the present decade. At worst they are seen as dangerous distortions or dilutions of the historic faith. Unless the Christian church is to become no more than a Society for the Preservation of the Privileged and the Prosperous, we cannot ignore liberation theologies. They are the church's harbingers of a most profound expression of agony and hope for the peoples of the Third World, the ethnic minorities of America, and the aspirations of women on a global scale.

This chapter has a modest goal, yet one that by no means can be taken for granted. I hope to show convincingly that paying attention to liberation theologies is of high importance to the church today, and that our

3

personal and collective relationship with Jesus Christ is deeply involved in our response to the alienated, the outcasts, and the relatively powerless. What you will be reading is essentially my own attempts to listen to liberation theologies and to comprehend the implications of their messages and methods for the Christian community, and thus for my own life as well.

Note what this chapter does *not* attempt. I do not speak *for* the Third World, nor for blacks or feminists. I do express what I believe they are saying to me and to other privileged and prosperous Christians. I do not attempt to offer a doctrinal study of the various theologies of liberation, although a number of themes and directions are discussed. Within Third World liberation theologies alone there are complex differences of emphasis. If we consider the combined variables and intricacies of Third World, ethnic, and feminist theologies, there are most likely few, if any, theologians capable of the comprehensive theological task of interpreting all three.

The Reality and Immensity of Human Suffering

To hear liberation theology is first of all to hear a message about *human suffering*. More than anything else initially, the word which I hear through the several liberation theologies is a message about *the intensity and the constancy of human suffering for the majority of the world's people*. Liberation theology is not a so-called ivory tower theology. On the contrary, taken as a whole, liberation theology wells up out of an experiential crucible: the misery of the majority.

The human suffering out of which liberation theologies arise is multi-dimensional. Held before us are the hungry and the virtually homeless multitudes of the earth. Liberation theology speaks from the experience of the outcasts, the people who lack what we call "the necessities of life." This impoverishment is the condition of daily experience for the masses of people in the southern hemisphere of the world. Third World liberation theology in particular addresses itself to these conditions. Ethnic theologies point to similar conditions for a significant percentage of Hispanic, Asian, Native, and black Americans.

A great deal of human suffering, however, takes place in a way that cannot be caught with the eye of a camera. The loss of human dignity, the absence of freedom of choice, the exclusion from participation in decision-making, the internalized erosion of self-respect—these are forms of human suffering that also represent the concern of theologies of liberation for the poor, for ethnic minorities, and for women throughout the world.

Widely quoted figures in church journals reveal the conditions of the world in this comparison: if the world were a village of 100 people, 70 of them would be unable to read, over 50 would be suffering from malnutrition, and over 80 would live in what we call substandard housing. Of the 100 members of the global village, 6 would be Americans. These 6 would have one-half of the village's entire income and would consume one-third of the total energy resources available. Of the U.S. population less than 2 percent would own 80 percent of the U.S. corporate wealth.

Liberation theologies are saying in various ways that any theology whose heart and soul is not caught up in the suffering of the majority is obsolete. James Cone, one of the most articulate voices of black theology in America, insists that the *point of departure* for Christian theology must be the condition of the oppressed and the necessity of their liberation.[2] Peruvian theologian Gustavo Gutiérrez quotes Edward Schillebeeckx as saying, "The church has for centuries devoted her attention to formulating truths and meanwhile did almost nothing to better the world. In other words, the church focused on orthodoxy and left orthopraxis in the hands of nonmembers and nonbelievers."[3]

Gutiérrez and other liberation theologians are asserting that the verification for Christian theology is whether or not it involves us in active, effective participation in the struggle of the oppressed for liberation. According to this claim, the most important authentication for the truth of Christian theology is not finally in a foolproof system of logic, not in labyrinthine arguments for the divinity of Christ or the existence of deity, and not in our church attendance nor in the efficacy of the sacraments. Liberation theologians are telling us that as far as they are concerned truth is much more than correct thought or doctrine, more than individual experiences which we label "religious," more than feelings, as important as all of these are. Only if Christian theology takes on the shape of God's liberating work in the world can it be called biblical theology. To liberation theologians, understanding the world is important only insofar as it leads to the struggle for transforming the world.

The first word I hear in liberation theologies is the reality and the immensity of human suffering. If that does not matter to us, we need not give credence to liberation theologies. If the suffering of others does matter to us, we cannot ignore a theology that calls us to listen, to care, and to respond.

A Major Source of Suffering: External Imposition

Liberation theology is more than a theology arising out of human suffering. It also is a theology deeply involved in historical homework. As

theologians of liberation—Third World, ethnic minority, and feminist[4]—
go about their tasks, they are carefully analyzing the *causes* of human
suffering. To be sure, suffering has many sources—natural and environmental misfortunes or handicaps, political tyranny within one's own
country, indigenous cultural conditions, and to some degree the limitations of human finitude itself.

Nevertheless, in analyzing the economic, political, and cultural factors
in historical development, liberation theologians have become increasingly exact in describing how a great deal of today's misery is an *imposed*
suffering. For example, if we do our homework on the history of Native
Americans since the coming of Europeans, it doesn't take long to discover
the root cause of today's deprivation among Native Americans. The long
sequence of unkept treaties by the United States government and the
widespread mutilation of Native American self-image, customs, and land
rights constitute a pattern of systemic genocide.

Because the history most of us have known has been written by the
powerful, the dominant, and the victors, only recently has the U.S. public
in general become aware of the degree to which the present situation of
Native Americans is due to imposed unjust conditions. The imposition of
suffering on the Native American is only one example, and this becomes
clear as we dare to open ourselves to a broader measure of historical
homework. It is because suffering is often imposed on the weak by the
strong that it is called *oppression* by liberation theologies. In many
instances the fact of oppression continues in policies and practices of
economic and political systems. In other situations the effects or consequences of oppression are still very much a factor in people's lives even
when the past policies of oppression are no longer given overt legal or
popular sanction.

To listen to black theologians of liberation is to become aware that the
oppressive conditions in which many black Americans live today are not
accidental nor the results of chance. We are part of a history and of a
resulting system today which, in spite of significant examples of progress,
continue to impose various forms of exploitation and suffering. For
example, recent census reports show the largest increase in the number
of poor people in the United States since the government began keeping
this set of statistics in 1959. The census bureau reported an increase of
25.9 million persons (approximately one person in eight) with incomes of
less than $5,500 a year. The government currently defines poverty level
as an income of $5,500 for a non-farm family of four. These millions
constitute a 10.7 percent increase over the previous year and the largest
jump in seventeen years. Blacks constitute 31 percent of the poor in the
nation, though they are less than 12 percent of the population. With a

growing disparity between the affluent and the poor in a nation that consumes nearly 40 percent of the world's goods, it is obvious that we seriously neglect the human factor in our system of life.[5]

In the 1970s the much talked about improvements of life for ethnic minorities in the United States have proven to be largely cosmetic. In spite of new civil rights laws, special ghetto programs, the War on Poverty, and stepped-up tokenist hiring, the plight of the vast majority of blacks and other ethnic minorities remains essentially the same.

During the past twenty-five years there has been virtually no permanent improvement in the relative economic position of blacks in America. Median black incomes have been fluctuating at a level between 47 percent and 60 percent of median white incomes. Segregation of neighborhoods has been steadily increasing in almost all cities. This is resulting in an ethnic minority inner city surrounded by an affluent circle of predominantly white suburbs. The rate of unemployment among blacks is generally twice as high as among whites, however, and this in turn has meant a smaller and smaller tax base for the central city school systems. Meanwhile blacks pay higher rents on inferior housing, higher prices in ghetto stores, and higher insurance premiums. To understand ethnic theologies of liberation is to realize that theology cannot be separated from the economically provoked suffering of the people.

Only in recent years, with the help of feminist theologians and writers, have I as a male become aware of the extent of discrimination against women, psychologically, socially, economically, culturally, and politically. When Christian theology is separated from an adequate historical grounding, it tends to overlook past and present impositions of suffering. On a universal scale, with a few cultural exceptions, women have been treated through the centuries as property or chattel at worst and as male appendages at best. The arduous struggles of women in the United States to gain the vote, to be recognized as persons in their own right, and to be ordained to ministry in the church amply testify to the imposition of unjust limits on women in the United States. An explosion of books and other literature in the past few years documents the exploitation of women and supports the rightful emergence of a liberation theology from a feminist perspective.

To become conversant with Third World theologians is to become painfully educated on the historical dominance of African, Asian, and Latin neighbors by the nations of the West. Once informed, it is not too difficult to come to terms personally with past oppression in terms of slavery, exploitation of the natural resources, or keeping the masses in servility without training in self-governance or in educational development. These things we know are part of the sordid history of colonialism and imperialism practiced by the so-called civilized Christian nations of the West.

What is more difficult, if we are to believe the claims of Third World theologians, is to come to grips with the *present* exploitation of Third World countries by a network of economic domination in which the United States government combines with the interests of large U.S. corporations. One of the major tasks for Christians in the United States is to do *our homework* so that we come to grips with the connection between our lifestyles and systems and the suffering of others. If the way we are developing the world is a causative factor in the suffering of others, we need to understand how this is so and take responsibility in whatever ways we can. If our economic system inevitably and irrevocably exploits the weak in other countries as well as our own, we need to have our ears opened and hear the prophetic Word of God. If our competitive economic system must become more human or even be replaced by a new system in order that persons be valued more than profits, the Christian community must respond under the Lordship of Jesus Christ. In Chapter Five we will have further opportunity to discuss this dilemma.

Exposing oneself to liberation theology is obviously not a form of armchair recreation. As a privileged and prosperous North American white male, I read theologies of liberation for one essential reason: to see myself and "my people" as others see us, in the light of actual history and in the light of the Christian message. There are other reasons but they are relatively insignificant. To see myself through the aperture of the hungry, the powerless, and the exploited is bound to be painful. Christian theology, however, has taught me that there can be rebirth through painful discovery, great promise in costly grace, and beatitude in dying to false securities. To see myself through the mirror of global history, to see the enforced exploitation of others through the workings of past and present systems is surely to be in touch with the living Lord of history.

Liberation theologians, each in his or her own context, are telling us that much human suffering is imposed or enforced by unjust structures and systems. Oppression is the name given to this fact. Liberation theologians are calling for an end to systemic oppression. If we take this seriously, it means a re-examination of our conformity and unquestioned trust in our present systems.

An Impressionistic Profile: Particularities and Contrasts

Calling for an end to imposed suffering constitutes a common characteristic of theologies of the oppressed. Yet it hardly provides a clue to the complexity of these theologies or to their differences. Nor will it suffice for our purpose to say simply that feminist theology is especially concerned with sexism, ethnic theology with racism, and Third World theology with classism or economic oppression.

Acknowledging that any treatment will be oversimplified that falls short of a full-scale research and book-length critique on *each* theology of liberation, I would like at least to attempt an impressionistic profile of my hearing. My hope is to convey the importance of listening to liberation theologies, that is, of making the effort, and further, of exposing one's hearing in both its accuracy and its distortions to continual testing and correction.

From *ethnic theologies* I hear a recovery of history, heroes, and heroines, with affirmation of one's own identity in that historical experience. Black writing, such as Alex Haley's *Roots,* has symbolized the uncovering of the black experience in America, with roots in African ancestors. This process of awareness has been a task of the black church in our time as it has sought to keep alive and to re-emphasize the lessons of black suffering and survival. The contributions of black worship, preaching, and art have come to the forefront.

The uncovering of history, heroes, and heroines has led to a sense of solidarity of those in the struggle for black liberation. The liberation movement, propelled by black theologians and by secular thinkers, has affirmed blackness as essential to speaking the truth. Centered in story rather than in theological systems, black theology connects the God of liberation with political and economic liberation in the here and now.

The kinship of ethnic, feminist, and Third World theologies is their common emphasis on hope. This embraces both the struggle for inner awareness and the affirmation of persons, and the movement toward a new political vision for society or humanity. The process by which hope comes alive and is shared takes different names: black (or Native American, or Hispanic-American) pride; conscientization (in Third World language); consciousness-raising (among feminists). The precise shape of the hoped for new order will vary even from writer to writer *within* any one of the three theologies of liberation. In spite of the variables, however, the future hope will have to do with people priorities in which human freedom and dignity are reflected in a more humane economic system, a better stewardship of ecological resources, and a political system sensitive to the powerless. For the most part ethnic theologies move beyond a desire to share in cultural affluence to the deeper questioning of the dominant white culture's values and priorities.

I hear ethnic theologies insisting on the distinctiveness of their history, experience, and present gifts in the broader spectrum of society. In effect I hear them saying, "We have been somebody, we are somebody, and we will be somebody—not just anybody, but the particular and distinctive people whom God has brought into being and with whom God is participating in a present-day Exodus from a marginal existence to become new subjects of history. As subjects of history rather than objects, we are aware of the political, economic, cultural, and historical contradictions of our existence. We are those people for whom God wills self-determination in order to give our gifts to humanity's history for the sake of a new world."

From *feminist theology* I hear and see a sisterhood community which, for the benefit of women and men alike, challenges role stereotypes (both feminine and masculine mystiques), calls for genuine personhood rather than a satellite or derivative existence, and longs for a Christian servant-hood born of choice rather than a servitude and submissiveness yoked to dependence. Feminist theologians are calling into radical question the world's most ancient and universal form of oppression, that of sexual caste and patriarchal domination.

Like ethnic theologies feminist theology addresses itself to the exorcism of debased self images that have been internalized.[6] From the strength of a new interiority and solidarity, feminist theology calls for a reconstructed society. Rosemary Ruether in particular does her theologizing with a constant view of the ecological crisis, or, as she puts it, our cosmic covenant as well as our social covenant. Our entire social and economic fabric will depend on how we handle our dwindling ecological resources.

Also like ethnic theology feminist theology is recovering a usable past in terms of examining the lessons of history, the validity of women's experience in their struggle with patriarchal dominance, and the heroines of church and society not previously given visibility by male history writers.

Whereas the emphasis within the previous women's rights movements tended to be equal opportunity within the existing system, advocates of women's liberation in the 1960s and 1970s have envisioned the necessity for a new system, recognizing that systems themselves are oppressive. "Changes in the condition of women depend on basic changes in society, its values and institutions. . . . The demand for equal participation in the working world is being raised at the same time that the nature of work and attitudes toward it are changing rapidly. . . . The dynamic of our movement will be to change our own lives and the institutions that oppress us."[7]

Feminist theology is similar to other theologies of liberation in calling for the freedom to participate in shaping one's own destiny, emphasizing the corporate and social nature of both sin and salvation and the role of the Christian community in identifying with the marginal, the powerless, and the outcast.

In *Third World theologies* the point of departure is not sexism or racism as such but the economic system in which I am a beneficiary and in which I participate. A hearing of Third World theology must state plainly that United States economic development is seen as an overriding factor in Third World oppression. It is the clear conviction of Third World theologians, especially those in Latin America, that in order to provide consumer goods for a relatively small affluent elite, globally speaking, the United States is using up the raw materials of the Third World, as well as its own, in unprecedented fashion. In addition, to expand this level of development is not to solve humanity's production problems, but rather to compound them, since we are failing to recognize the exhaustible capacity of "natural capital."[8] Thus, the assumption that U.S.-style economic development for the masses in Third World countries is either taking place or is even desirable has been called into radical question. The myth of development, then, as either factual or desirable is a cardinal tenet of much Third World theology.

The exploitive and wasteful nature of U.S. consumption, clearly a destruction of the world's ecological resources if applied on a global scale, has led Third World theologians to be highly critical of American capitalism. In contrast with New Testament themes of solidarity, sharing, and sacrifice, capitalism is experienced by the masses of people in the Third World as dehumanizing, exploitive, and wasteful. Given the miserable living conditions of so many Third World people, and given the fact that capitalism is experienced by them as a boon for the ruling minority and a bane to the masses, we should not be surprised when they cast their hopes in the direction of a socialist design for improvement of their own societies as well as the world order.

Perhaps the most significant source of Third World theology for me has been the work of José Míguez Bonino, a Protestant theologian from Argentina. In his *Doing Theology in a Revolutionary Situation* he traces the sixteenth-century Spanish conquest and colonialization of much of Latin America, followed by the nineteenth-century modernization, or development. The latter is a euphemism for neocolonialism, featuring cheap labor, raw materials, and economic dependence.

> The basic fact of the determination of all our economy and development by the needs and problems of the masters prevailing at the time (whether British or American) is in all cases the same. The much better known and often condemned political and military interventions of the United States in Latin America are only the necessary maneuvers for the protection of this economic relation.[9]

While most Christians in the U.S. will have their difficulties accepting these views and believing the facts that support them, few among us have escaped at least occasional struggle with the conflict between the New Testament's emphasis on cooperation and mutuality and capitalism's demand for profits and the corresponding necessity for growth in production and consumption. This point will surface again in Chapter Five.

Another element that I hear in Third World writings, especially prominent in the work of Brazilian educator Paulo Freire, is conscientization. As already pointed out, conscientization is an educational process by which the powerless and deprived become aware of themselves and their situation, including the political, economic, and cultural contradictions which deny them their humanness, and act to bring about change. The undergirding concept is that education must be a humanizing activity rather than training for conformity to existing powers and principalities.

Additional concerns in the writings of Third World theologians are the necessity for radical change in the social structure, with displacement of the ruling elite; the shaping of a new system that fits the needs of a particular nation rather than being simply a carbon copy from elsewhere; the emergence of a new participation by the people in their own destiny; and the disparagement of traditional charity and liberal reformism as socially irrelevant.

Basic to these theologies is the biblical notion that there is one history and one Lord over all of history. Gustavo Gutiérrez is especially lucid in holding together reconciliation with God, socio-political struggle, and human maturity as one single reality. Like other Third World theologians he believes that Exodus represents the unity between the redemptive and the socio-political dimensions of God's liberating action, a liberation fulfilled in Jesus Christ.

Even a cursory outline of Third World theology would be grievously deficient without calling attention to the remarkable changes taking place in the Latin American church, and especially the Roman Catholic church. Almost weekly I read of new sufferings and persecutions of Roman Catholic priests and religious throughout Latin America, as well as lay persons. The recent history of these changes is a drama of present day martyrdom and surely constitutes one of the most far-reaching acts of God in our history.[10]

Contrasts and Conflicts

The contrasts and conflicts in liberation theologies are no less significant than the points of compatibility. These differences help us to understand the nuances of each one and to appreciate the particular historical variables from which each arises. After all, oppression is never oppression in general, but always in particular. Differences among liberation movements may be illustrated by the following convictions from a minority woman, a view that will also vary among minorities:

> The seeds which spawn the racist mentality also spawn the sexist mentality, though the results differ in both their historical manifestations and degree of oppression. White women must realize that minority women are intrinsically bound to the total struggle of race. The enemy (for minority women) is "the white establishment," not her man. . . . Minority men and women do need to work out new supportive and freeing roles with each other, but that will have to happen within the context of the struggle for justice in America. White women must learn to trust their minority sisters.[11]

Similarly, women may be concerned about patriarchal oppression in Latin America; Third World people may see North American women, and for that matter affluent minority males as well, as participants in an economic system that oppresses Latin America. In other words, complex histories and present forms of oppression mean that in a certain context the oppressed of one group will be seen as oppressors by another group. This fact is a reminder of the many faces and forms of oppression, and that God's judgment/redemption is a universal reality. "To recognize structures of oppression within our own group . . . would force us to deal with ourselves, not as simply oppressed or oppressors, but as people who are sometimes one and sometimes the other in different contexts. A more mature and chastened analysis of the capacities of human beings for good and evil would flow from this perception."[12]

I believe that the only way to become truly conversant with the richness of liberation theologies in all of their similarities and contrasts is to spend time and effort in studying them, and more important, to live them in ministry. The works in the notes for this chapter would be a very modest beginning for study.

Liberation as a Central Biblical Theme

Liberation theology is more than reflection on the past and present experience of people who suffer. It is more than a socio-political analysis of systems and structures of oppression, and more than historical homework. Theologians and church leaders such as Gustavo Gutiérrez,

Juan Segundo, Letty Russell, José Míguez Bonino, Helder Camara, Abel Muzorewa, Rosemary Ruether, and James Cone critically reflect on the realities of suffering and oppression *in the light of the Christian Gospel.* A common affirmation of liberation theologians, whatever their differences, is that the God of Scripture is a God whose activity is the liberation of the weak, the outcast, and the abused. In other words, liberation theologians understand themselves to be speaking from a biblical grounding in identifying the Christian indicative and imperative with historical liberation. The liberation of the Israelites from bondage under Pharaoh is a key paradigm or model of the liberating God. Jesus Christ is proclaimed as God's liberating savior who identifies his ministry and message in special ways with the have-nots and the exploited. The church's identification with the disinherited is not an optional matter, but a task constitutive of the church's very meaning.

In Chapter Two we will look at the sense in which God's partiality to the cause of the weak and the powerless is a recurring biblical motif. Here it will be enough to assert that liberation is seen by liberation theologians as a cardinal biblical focus. The message is not only that there is widespread suffering and deprivation due to imposed limits, but also that God is leading the forces of liberation. In the Appendix we will reflect critically on the claims of liberation theologians, including the use of the term "liberation" and its biblical grounding.

Liberation From and Liberation For

In conversations on liberation theology people sometimes ask, "What does liberation theology affirm?" The question is predicated on the awareness that liberation theology is *against* imposed suffering or oppression in its many forms: subhuman living conditions, the inability to influence one's own destiny, the indignities of exclusion, the dehumanizing influence of racial myths and sexist stereotypes. There is less certainty, however, on what liberation is for, that is, after liberation, what then? What is God's purpose in liberation?

Because of the extent of human suffering, liberation theology spotlights the alleviation of existing wrongs. History is re-examined and surgical questions are raised. Where suffering abounds, liberation theology speaks of extricating human beings from the situation and opposes the existing conditions. On a recent summer vacation our family saw a young hitchhiker on the outskirts of a large city. His sign said only, "Out of here!" Liberation theologians are first of all saying, "Out of this situation."

This fact, however, should not obscure the future orientation that is basic in a variety of ways to all liberation theology. Although the vision of the kingdom of God will vary and the pulsebeat of hope will utilize a range of images, all Christian liberation theologies are based on a vision of God's liberating grace for the future of a re-created humanity. As I try to hear what liberation theologians are saying about the purposes of God's liberating grace, it has to do with a new community of human beings.

Liberation is for a redeemed community, for a new solidarity among human beings. Liberation means the removal of oppressive conditions so that there can be genuine communion with God and with humanity. Freedom from slavery through the Exodus event is freedom for a new humanity rather than merely a privatistic relationship with God in isolation from others. Gustavo Gutiérrez emphasizes the theme of a new humanity, the communion of human beings with God and among themselves. The creation of a new humanity is the work that Christ seeks to bring to fulfillment.[13] Letty Russell also emphasizes this theme when she speaks of the Old Testament concept of salvation as *shalom,* a personal yet social wholeness and well-being. Without denying that salvation includes the message of individual deliverance from sin and death, liberation theologies place emphasis on the total goal of salvation which is the gift of shalom (complete social and physical wholeness and harmony.)[14] J. Deotis Roberts in *Liberation and Reconciliation: A Black Theology,* speaks in a similar vein: "Liberation moves toward community, not chaos; toward reconciliation between equals."[15]

In other words, the aim of liberation is not only freedom from the tyranny of grinding poverty and dehumanizing exploitation. Liberation is freedom to participate in a new humanity of justice, wholeness, and dignity. It is precisely this new freedom that liberation theologians see as the work of God in history as expressed in both Old and New Testaments.

The Methods of Liberation Theology

When I was a student in Union Theological Seminary, New York, in 1957-58, one of our mentors was the late Paul Scherer. He was a master teacher and a superb preacher of the Word. I had come to Union with several other graduates of Perkins School of Theology, where we had been influenced by the so-called existentialist method of theology. With an abiding respect for Dr. Scherer two or three of us used to debate the appropriate beginning place for sermons (as if there were only one!). Our existentialist view was prone to begin with some dimension of the human condition, followed by an application of the Christian message.

Dr. Scherer would unmercifully caricature our approach by saying, "You paint me in a corner and then trot out Jesus as THE answer! You've got it exactly reversed. You should ordinarily begin with some passage or reference to Good News and then go from there into the human situation." We claimed that Romans, as one example, began with the human predicament (chapter 1, verse 18 and following). Scherer countered, "You conveniently skip the first seventeen verses which begin with the Good News." Our answer was that these initial verses were a mere prologue and not constitutive of the basic message! To this day I am grateful to this giant of the Word for opening our eyes to *more than one way* to shape our homilies!

Fortunately, Christian theologizing through the years has utilized a variety of methods for its tools. Theological and homiletical approaches have frequently begun with the assertion of good news from Scripture or tradition, and proceeded to deduce various tenets of faith for Christian living. Liberation theologies, however, tend to begin with the human condition rather than the announcement of good news in a vacuum. The life experience of the people is characteristically the "point of departure," as Cone has identified it, for liberation theologians. The experience of the majority I have described as imposed suffering or oppression.

Letty Russell indicates one of the basic methods of liberation theology by saying that in general liberation theologies stress an inductive rather than a deductive approach. In the past much theology was done by deducing conclusions from first principles established out of Christian tradition. The inductive method draws material for reflection from life experience as it relates to the gospel message.[16] Thus, liberation theologies take into account situational variables which speak concretely to particular needs. The point of departure for liberation theologies is the condition of oppressed peoples and the necessity of liberation.

Constantly Revised Questions

As an inductive process, liberation theologies tend to be inquiring and experimental. Letty Russell calls it "a theology of constantly revised questions."[17] Doctrine, images, and language are all submitted to the testing of a more inclusive human experience. Patriarchal presuppositions are exposed as partial and patronizing expressions of the Gospel. Privatistic interpretations of salvation are called into question by theologians who claim, "To preach the universal love of God is inevitably to go against all injustice, privilege, oppression, or narrow nationalism."[18]

The clay feet of many heroes and heroines of Christian tradition are revealed through the disturbing questions of liberation theologians. Why did Luther ruthlessly put down the peasants' rebellion? Why did his theology of grace not apply more redemptively to the poor? Why have so many white theologians through the years hardly dealt with the reality of ethnic minority suffering? And what does it mean that so many leading male theologians have assumed first-class citizenship for men and a secondary role for women? The questions of liberation theologies reveal the cultural conditioning of biblical writers and our predecessors in the faith. These questions also unmask our own prejudices today.

Corporate Theologizing

Theology in liberation style, as I understand it, is by and large a corporate experience. Because it draws on the experience of a group of persons, the theologian is dependent on the people in a special way for his or her data. While any Christian theologian is rightfully dependent on the Christian community past and present for theologizing, the liberation theologian of today is likely to be part of an oppressed community and sees theology out of that experience and with the support of that community. "Such an approach is heavily dependent on the corporate support of the community out of which it grows. . . . Feminist theology grows out of small communities of women experimenting together in actions and reflections."[19]

Corporate theologizing means, too, that the experience of laypersons becomes a decisive factor in the shaping of theology. Theologians draw not only from other theologians, but from the life experiences of oppressed people. Furthermore, corporate theologizing means that theologians do their work increasingly in conversation with historians, sociologists, and other disciplines of thought and discovery. The contextual theology is not isolated from other fields of inquiry, but is partially dependent on them for doing theology.

I began this chapter suggesting that liberation theology could not be ignored by the Christian community. Actually you know and I know that we *can* ignore it in our comfortable churches and in our comfortable lives. The point is that if we do ignore liberation theology we will be hard pressed to call ourselves the *Christian* community. For the Christian community is derived from Jesus Christ, and Jesus Christ, the Universal Lord of all, is the very particular champion of the world's untouchables.

As we turn to Chapter Two, I want to reflect on a theme of Scripture that for years has intrigued, troubled, and uplifted me. I believe it is integral to liberation theology.

CHAPTER TWO

The Anatomy of Liberation:
The Foolishness of God

When Saint Paul School of Theology was in the process of interviewing me for its presidency, the Search Committee requested that I offer the names of four references. After a certain amount of deliberation, I offered the names of a United Methodist Bishop, a black District Superintendent, a prominent theologian, and the woman who was the immediate past board chairperson of the church that I was then serving. Thinking that I had responded with an impressive list that "covered the waterfront," I awaited the committee's reply.

Before long they came by appointment to my study and informed me that they had interviewed each of the references I had provided. They then said to me, "Now we would like to interview your congregation's custodian to hear what he or she has to say about you." I was deeply impressed by the candor and insight behind this request, as much so in fact as anything in the entire interview process. Revealed in that one episode was the seminary's concern for all people and for a just use of power in relation to them.

What does this incident have to do with liberation theology? In my judgment it reflects something of the reversal of conventional wisdom that is so typical of the biblical narratives. In terms of human wisdom the Gospel is for the most part an absurdity. I use the term "absurdity" not in the sense of the theater of the absurd, nor in the sense that it defies rational logic. The Gospel is absurd in the sense that it is the world's wisdom upside down and inside out. The Christian Word is the world's word in reverse, sharply contrasting with the standards and norms of

19

conventional worldly wisdom. In biblical terms the absurdity of God's Word is what Paul calls the foolishness of God.

God's Foolishness: 1 Corinthians 1

I regard Paul's articulation of God's foolishness in his first chapter to the Corinthians (1 Cor. 1:18-31) to be an indispensable illustration for an adequate grasp of how Scripture as a whole tends to function. Knowing that writers are forever choosing one hobby-horse text and squeezing it to death, I nevertheless hope to show that this Pauline text is representative of who God is and what God does throughout the biblical story. In the service of this task, I will draw the reader into this passage for a moment, and then follow up with a sampling of other supporting biblical material—images, symbols, and stories.

Through the evidence gathered by biblical scholars, we know that Paul was writing to a Corinthian church made up largely of slaves and freed persons. Paul tells them that the foolishness of God is wiser than human beings and the weakness of God is stronger than human beings. God has made foolish the wisdom of the world and in fact is destroying the wisdom of the wise. Verses 26-31 are particularly striking. The Corinthians are told that although their worldly credentials are next to nothing, "God chose what is foolish in the world to shame the wise, God chose what is weak in the world to shame the strong, God chose what is low and despised in the world to bring to nothing things that are, so that no human being might boast in the presence of God" (vv. 27-29). *The Good News Bible* translates verse 28: "God chose what the world looks down on, and despises, and thinks is nothing, in order to destroy what the world thinks is important." *The New English Bible* translates the same verse, "God has chosen things low and contemptible, mere nothings, to overthrow the existing order."

When Paul uses the terms "foolish," "weak," "low," and "despised," to what is he referring? Is he speaking of the cross, that is, of Christ Jesus crucified? Or is he referring to the Corinthians themselves? I believe there is a sense in which he is speaking of both, certainly so if the entire text (vv. 18-31) is considered. The crucified Christ is never far from Paul's mind. The cross constitutes the backdrop for virtually everything he articulates. The cross is folly, yet the power of God. The cross is not the long sought sign expected in messianic activity, and it is certainly not the wisdom of philosophers. The Crucified One is a stumbling block, an absurdity according to the major religious expectations and the secular wisdom of the age. In short the cross is the foolishness of God.

In verses 26-29, however, it seems evident that Paul is referring to the Corinthians *themselves* as the foolish, the weak, and the despised. After all, who were they in the Roman Empire? Who were they to anyone, except themselves and God? Their place is the same place as the cross: nowhere, except in God's sight. This passage is like a rerun of God's *choice* in the Old Testament where Semitic slaves are chosen for God's mission to the wider world.

Once again, according to this text, God is choosing the powerless, the positionless, the people without status or credentials, to point to the ultimate reality of God's love, now made explicit in the crucified Christ. The folly of the cross becomes the source of our wisdom, our righteousness, and our sanctification. God's freedom to choose anybody at any place and time is a characteristic mark of the biblical understanding of history.

The Metabolism of Scripture

When we look at the pitiful plight of the Israelites in Egyptian bondage, we can only conclude that they would have been last on the list of conventional human wisdom for any significant mission to the world. With God they were first on the list. Thoughout the Old Testament we see the most unlikely persons chosen for God's tasks. The list includes Sarah, who as an old woman gave birth to Isaac; Moses, a murderer with a speech impediment; the widow of Zarephath, who provided food for Elijah in spite of her poverty; Deborah, a prophetess victorious in battle; Jeremiah, a youth with no track record in prophetic activity; and Amos, an unknown shepherd from Tekoa. The foolishness of God is also revealed in the remarkable concept of the Suffering Servant in Isaiah 53.

The New Testament story is no different in this respect. The disciples and followers of Jesus were for the most part "Corinthian types," who, though not slaves to the Romans, were not distinguished in any way whatsoever by status of birth or by worldly wisdom, power, or achievement.

Thus, the Corinthian theme of God's foolishness is not an isolated one. To be truly conversant with Scripture is to be aware that God's foolishness, which reverses so much of human wisdom, is more like the metabolism of Scripture itself. To comprehend what liberation theologies are about, one needs to get in touch with the recurring theme of God's foolishness. To do so is to touch the anatomy of liberation.

Before examining what the theme of God's foolishness portends for us, I want to suggest how this theme surfaces throughout the Bible in images, symbols, and stories. The language of Scripture frequently uses images that have the quality of foolishness, weakness, and utter reversal of the present order. "Every valley will be lifted up, and every mountain be made low" (Isa. 53: 4). "Many that are first will be last, and the last first" (Mark 10: 31). "He who finds his life will lose it , and he who loses his life for my sake will find it" (Matt. 10: 39). "For everyone who exalts himself will be humbled, and he who humbles himself will be exalted" (Luke 14:11). While each passage deserves study in its particular context in order to arrive at its meaning, it can be said that the wisdom of the world is reversed and turned upside down.

The same quality of absurdity characterizes virtually all Christian symbols. From crib to carpenter's bench to the crown of thorns and the cross, the faith symbols can strike one only as foolish and absurd by secular calibration. If we had not been drawn into the tradition of the faith and were to assemble these symbols initially from scratch, would not our first impression be either disbelief or cynicism? Precisely because these symbols are familiar to us, they need to strike us all over again with their foolish ultimacy. A loaf of bread. A chalice. The clue to life? Surely this is nonsense! Only it gets worse! A water basin. Water. A towel. A cross. An empty tomb. Could we deliberately choose symbols that contrast more radically with existing cultural assumptions and practices?

When we look at the Christian story through representative episodes of events and tradition, the one fact that stands out is the absurdity of it all in worldly terms. To begin with, the birth. The Lord of Lords and King of Kings is born in a manger, not in the palace of Pilates and Herods. Choose almost any of Jesus' teachings. Even allowing for the oral period of transmission, the time of written fragments, and the fact that we see Jesus through the eyes of the evangelists and the early church, there remains an absolutely absurd quality permeating his utterances. The people of Jesus' time had heard the word of hate for one's enemy. That is our society's word, too. Love your enemies and pray for those who persecute you! What does human wisdom do with that?

His Word is that the kingdom of God is at hand. God is in your midst with promise and claim, so live now, receiving life as a brand new gift. Our word is that you can live only if the circumstances are right or if events turn out the way we "if" them. His Word is the word of acceptance, validating our worth as a sheer gift. It is the word of justification by God's grace. Our word is the performance principle, with gods of production, promotion, and prestige. His Word is that our greatest beatitude is in feeding the hungry and befriending the homeless, for in so doing we experience ourselves, our neighbor, and our God at the deepest level. Our word is the mania for worldly recognition and for avoiding the cries of the have-nots. Associating with them won't get you anywhere!

If we take the beatitudes from Matthew's version of the Sermon on the Mount as reasonably typical of Jesus' teachings, we are looking at the world's word in reverse, especially as applied to male customs and expectations. Blessed are the poor in spirit (those who acknowledge their need for God's gifts): a conflict with the basic presuppositions of the masculine mystique. Blessed are those who mourn; a conflict with our long-standing tradition of bottling up our feelings and of denying our grief. Blessed are the merciful; a contradiction to our eye-for-an-eye custom. Blessed are the peacemakers; we offer accolades to those who have successfully waged war, but how many citizens have received medals from the government for waging peace? To top it all, and yet a confirmation of it all, the absurdity of self-giving love nailed on a wooden crossbeam.

God's Foolishness: What Does It Mean?

God's foolishness, as proclaimed by Paul in 1 Corinthians, and as expressed in countless ways throughout Scripture, comes to us as a gift of affirmation and acceptance. We all have the same starting and ending point, regardless of differences in theology, politics, nationality, race, sex, or any other human differentiation. This means that you do not have to have the right membership card to have a place and a part in God's work. In the eyes of God we are all "Corinthians," that is, without impressive credentials and qualifications. When we are despairing of whether or not our lives can serve a useful or meaningful purpose, the Word of God's foolish freedom to choose the weak and the low puts us on our feet again with hope born of a God-centered self-esteem.

On the other hand, God's foolishness can appear as a judgment on our cleverness and our so-called success. To those of us in the world of relative affluence, achievement, and power, God's absurd Word is a Word over and against us in order to be *for* us! Reminding us of what enormous failures we can become in our successes, the foolishness of God brings us to our knees. In the Vietnams and Watergates of our time, the foolishness of God is indeed destroying the wisdom of the worldly wise. Our brightest and best are not as wise as God's foolishness, nor are they as strong as God's weakness. The most basic assumptions and practices of our consumer-oriented society are being destroyed in our own time by the wisdom of God. The very foundations of economic growth and of an unlimited standard of living for a few are now exposed as a bittersweet second at best and as utter folly at worst. For we now have to recognize the exhaustible nature of nature's resources.

When we lose the sense of the Gospel's absurdity, we begin to remake the Gospel in our own image. What we then call "gospel" takes on the coloration of our values instead of the polychromatic colors of global consciousness and the polyphonic sounds of the universal Gospel. We lose the wonder, the challenge, the risk, and, yes, even the deepest comfort of the Gospel. When we are blind to God's redemptive foolishness, we have traded the truth for a mess of accommodated, acculturated, adapted, and well-adjusted pottage. When we can no longer distinguish between our foolishness and God's foolishness, God has become no more than a casual accoutrement for the religiosity of the people.

The awareness of God's redemptive foolishness is the assurance of a divine discontent in our lives. Without the divine discontent there may be a placebo of the mind, but there can be no peace of mind in the sense of God's peace and joy. The absurdity of the Gospel is the Gospel's wisdom and its power to rescue us from a malaise of the spirit for a new freedom for others; to keep alive a vision of hope and a beatitude amid suffering; to challenge our conformist compulsions with the courage of an Isaiah or a Stephen; to motivate us for our best efforts to make the world a different world, and yet to reserve our primary celebration not for that effort itself, but for the eternal love which sustains and re-creates all such efforts.

In terms of my own witness to the faith, I must say that without a sense of the Divine Foolishness, the business of the church quickly becomes a boring opiate. *With* an awareness of and openness to the absurd Word in our midst, the work of the Christian community is the most exciting task in the world.

God's Foolishness and Liberation Theology

As we have seen, the foolishness of God contradicts worldly wisdom and ways. One New Testament scholar, John Dominic Crossan, has described some of Jesus' parables as "parables of reversal." Another writer puts it this way:

In the world of the Bible everything is turned upside down. The whole hierarchy of human values and the ladders of human greatness and self-importance are inverted or collapsed. All normal expectations, and the clever stratagems of the prudent are baffled. . . . This is not, however, a simple exchange of top for bottom, of reason for irrationality, of knowledge for ignorance. Rather, everything becomes topsy-turvy so that everything may be righted.[1]

With this in mind one has little difficulty in relating Divine Foolishness with the concerns of liberation theologies. The Divine Discontent portends an ultimate judgment "against all that is proud and lofty, against all that is lifted up and high, against every high tower and against every fortified wall" (Isa. 2). The foolishness of God is the biblical wellspring of liberation theology because God is clearly the God for whom the outcasts, the homeless, and the oppressed are a special concern.

One of the claims of liberation theology that has been particularly troublesome for privileged and prosperous Christians is that God takes sides and is therefore partial to or "on the side of " the poor and the powerless. Our brief study of Paul's first chapter in 1 Corinthians, as well as the other biblical references to God's foolishness, helps us to understand the sense in which God is biased in favor of the poor. Further light is shed by John C. Bennett in *The Radical Imperative:*

> God's love for all persons implies a strategic concentration on the victims of society, on the weak, the exploited, the neglected persons who are a large majority of the human race. . . . I use the word "strategic" because I do not believe that God loves the victims more than he does the beneficiaries of our institutions. . . . It seems clear to me that an emphasis on divine partiality understood in this strategic sense is an implication of the story of the last judgment in Matt. 25. . . . The identification of Christ with the hungry, the stranger or refugee, the naked, the sick, the imprisoned. . . .[2]

God's Partiality in the Old Testament

Throughout the Bible God's partiality in the strategic sense mentioned by Bennett is clearly present. In this section I will present a few selective examples from the Old Testament. The following section will provide similar illustrations from the New Testament. All of these serve to remind us of God's special care, identification, and action for the poor and the oppressed—a major focus of liberation theologies. From what has already been said, I trust that I will not be misunderstood when I suggest that Scripture typically reveals an "underdog" theology, to use a well-known phrase.

In the law, the Psalmists, and the prophets there are plentiful examples of God's strategic identification. In Leviticus 25 the jubilee passage requires the return of all land without compensation to the original owners every fiftieth year because "the land is mine (God's)." The jubilee was to prevent extremes of wealth and poverty among God's people, and thus constituted God's concern for the economic well-being of all. Related passages specify the proper response "if your brother becomes poor." In Deuteronomy 15 the code of law calls for meeting the needs of the poor by either lending or giving sufficiently to the need. This particular passage concludes, "You shall open wide your hand to your brother, to the needy and to the poor in the land" (15:11).

The salient point of the Old Testament law code in relation to the needs of the poor is this: to care for the poor is not an optional matter but instead integral to being in covenant with God. The protection of the poor is provided in numerous passages in both Leviticus and Deuteronomy. This protection ranges from interest-free loans to the remission of debts every seventh year to the prevention of family property loss.

God's concern for the poor is abundantly expressed in the Psalms. "Because the poor are despoiled, because the needy groan, I will now arise," says the Lord; "I will place him in the safety for which he longs" (Ps. 12:5). "I will satisfy her poor with bread" (Ps. 132:15). One of the most impressive testimonies to God's action on behalf of the weak and the afflicted is Psalm 82. In this remarkable passage God (Yahweh) brings judgment in the council of gods because they are not doing their job: to give justice to the weak and the fatherless, to maintain the right of the afflicted and the destitute, and to deliver the weak and the needy from the hand of the wicked. God's judgment is that the errant gods shall die like human beings. The decisive point seems to be that the very name "God" points to the reality who actively works on behalf of the weak and destitute. This is the *meaning* of the word "God" and the way that word functions for at least this segment of Old Testament tradition.

That God is a God of justice and of active love for the outcasts is not difficult to find in the prophets. A few citations will suffice. A powerful example is found in the message of Amos, who brings scathing judgment and a call to repentance because the needy have been crushed and justice has been thwarted. A stronger bond between God and the oppressed can hardly be conceived by the human mind than Amos' denunciation of social injustices and his advocacy of the rights of the poor.

Likewise, the prophet Isaiah repeatedly pronounces God's judgment on the idols of the people and the pride that they represent. The Lord of hosts is exalted in justice, for the Lord is a God of justice. "When the poor and needy seek water and there is none, and their tongue is parched with thirst, I the Lord will answer them, I the God of Israel will not forsake them" (41:17). Isaiah 58, which reinterprets the Lord's fast from a cultic, ascetic act to an ethical act, is one of the most convincing and moving passages of God's solidarity with the oppressed of the earth.

In these passages and in many others like them in the Old Testament, God is the champion of the poor and powerless. I will have more to say in Chapter Four about Isaiah 58 and the Old Testament's attitudes toward property and wealth. I have read enough Scripture, however, to wonder if people really know what they are saying when they exclaim, "What we need is to get back to the Bible!"

God's Partiality in the New Testament

Like the Old Testament, the New Covenant is characterized by God's special and strategic identification with human suffering. Especially in the gospel of Luke is this identification pronounced. Firmly rooted in the events that prepare for Jesus' coming is the Magnificat (Luke 1:46-55). It has been called one of the Bible's most revolutionary or radical passages. "God has scattered the proud in the imagination of their hearts, he has put down the mighty from their thrones, and exalted those of low degree; he has filled the hungry with good things, and the rich he has sent empty away" (vv. 51-53).

With this preface we are not surprised that in Luke's gospel Jesus from the beginning identifies his purpose with the poor and the oppressed. In his opening sermon at Nazareth he uses the Isaiah 61:1-2 text: "The Spirit of the Lord is upon me, because he has anointed me to preach good news to the poor. He has sent me to proclaim release to the captives and recovering of sight to the blind, to set at liberty those who are oppressed, to proclaim the acceptable year of the Lord" (Luke 4:18-19). Throughout the gospel of Luke Jesus fulfills this mission. Other typical passages include, "Go and tell John what you have seen and heard. . . . The poor have good news preached to them" (7:23); the parable of the Rich Fool (12:13-21); the Rich Man and Lazarus (16:19-31).

From many examples of Jesus' teachings—to say nothing of his personal association with outcasts and women and lepers—the most unforgettable and undeniable identification with the wretched and the powerless is located in the well-known Last Judgment account in Matthew 25:31-46. Here Jesus is so identified with the poor and needy that response, or lack of response, to them is also done to him. From this narrative one cannot avoid the conclusion that for those who belong to the community of Jesus, identification with the hungry, the homeless, and the outcast is neither optional nor peripheral, but primary and basic.

The response of the disciples to Jesus' call for participation in a sharing community, as well as the practice of the Jerusalem church and other Christian communities mentioned in the New Testament, will be part of our discussion in Chapter Four. The contents of this chapter, I hope, have established a clear link between the foolishness of God, liberation theology, and God's strategic partiality or functional identification with the people of the world who are forced to live a marginal existence.

Our journey now will lead us to explore how liberation theologies might be transposed into a theology for privileged and prosperous Christians. The focus will begin to move from what others have been saying to us, or at least what I have heard them saying to us with my imperfect ears, to what a liberation theology for us might sound like. Thus, our pilgrimage will take on a greater degree of interiority and, to some extent, autobiography.

PART TWO

Liberation Theology
for Privileged and
Prosperous Christians

CHAPTER THREE

The Blessed Disturbance in the Blessed Assurance

So far I have attempted to provide a listening instrument to enable privileged and prosperous Christians to pick up the pulse beat of Third World, black, and feminist liberation theologies. With this background I am ready now to explore where a liberation theology might begin for privileged and prosperous Christians. A variety of biblical images will be utilized as we seek to translate liberation theology into our own life situation. Reference to the gospel of Mark's account of the Gerasene Demoniac (Mark 5:1-20) will be especially useful.

A Neglected Dimension of Our Biblical Heritage: Critical Love

One of the generally accepted notions of our society is that to love is to be uncritical. This popular assumption was advertised, for example, on bumper stickers during the Vietnam War: "America—Love It or Leave It." The inherent presupposition in the message is that to love our country means to be uncritical of the administration's policy. To criticize or to call into question is to be disloyal or unloving or un-American. Either be noncritical or get out!

These assumptions are sometimes nurtured in cultural movements that seek to actualize human potential. The widespread popularity of Transactional Analysis as a helpful tool for human growth reveals the enormous need for a sense of acceptance and self-understanding. I'm O.K. and you're O.K. No human being can fulfill her or his potential apart from the reality of self-acceptance or a sense of self-worth. In spite of the excellent contributions of T.A., however, in some cases okayness has come to

31

mean that we do not call into question, we do not criticize or challenge, we do not rock the boat. Love is interpreted as a manifesto for agreement. The dimension of new inquiry, of searching out our differences, of probing new frontiers is surrendered in the name of togetherness and acceptance. If everybody and everything is O.K., it may make us feel good, but it will hardly lead to the discovery of depth in relationships or improvements in a society in which there is much that is not O.K. Too often our society is stretched between the antagonistic forces of uncritical lovers and unloving critics.

The biblical heritage is rich and profound in its combination of judgment and mercy, that is, of critical love. Although even biblical theologians have sometimes labeled the Old Testament as primarily judgmental and the New Testament as majoring in mercy, this simplistic testamental distinction is an inaccurate one. The intensity of so-called judgment in Matthew 23 and the depth of God's mercy in the Book of Hosea are only two illustrations to the contrary. As we look at the history of Israel, the most prominent dynamic is the judgment-mercy of God that calls Israel into being through the Exodus event, calls the covenant people into question over their idolatry, forgives them, and offers a new future.

God's judgment, even in its harshest form, is always merciful in the sense that it calls Israel away from its own bent toward idolatry and self-centeredness. God's mercy is always judgmental in that it presupposes that no other God is ultimate or worthy of ultimate devotion. To be sure, what we have come to label as judgment or mercy will be a prevailing motif in a specific passage. When the prophets pronounce woes on Israel and other nations, we call this God's judgment of the people. But the *intent* is clear, namely, that Israel turn away from a futile purpose to the life-giving covenant with God. Judgment is God's way of showing mercy. Otherwise the people would be abandoned to their bondage and unfaithfulness to God, neighbor, and self.

Likewise, God's mercy is a form of judgment. For example, reflect on a text like "God so loved the world that he gave his only Son, that whoever believes in him should not perish but have eternal life. For God sent the Son into the world, not to condemn the world, but that the world might be saved through him" (John 3:16-17). To be saved through Jesus Christ, however, is not to be "okay" to do anything we want to do . . . such as acts that are racist, sexist, or imperialistic. To believe in Jesus Christ is to love God and to love our neighbor in the world, both near and far away. Indeed, the text from John's gospel goes on to say, "And this is the judgment, that the light has come into the world, and men loved darkness rather than light, because their deeds were evil" (John 3:19).

Granted that as Christians we understand ourselves to be justified or "okayed" by faith in God's grace through Jesus Christ, it is also true that faith in Jesus Christ inevitably involves certain postures and stances toward life and toward other people. To say otherwise is to say that faith is strictly privatistic and devoid of ethical imperatives. It is true that if we love God or Christ, we are not bound to preconceived particularities of programs for social change nor legalistic predetermined specifics in human relationships. On the other hand it is also true that to do certain things is *not* to love God or Christ. If we do not care about the plight of hungry or downtrodden people, we do not love God or Jesus Christ. "If anyone says, 'I love God,' and hates his brother, he is a liar; for he who does not love his brother whom he has seen, cannot love God whom he has not seen" (1 John 4:20).

The biblical tradition offers a Good News that is communicated in a remarkable and diverse assortment of words. The vocabulary includes words like "salvation," "redemption," "reconciliation," "liberation," "wholeness," "justification," "sanctification," "freedom," "release," "deliverance," "healing," and "new creation." While Good News defined in these terms comes as a gift, this Good News does not come from just any God. The Good News comes from a very particular God of History who through the law, the prophets, and Jesus Christ has identified with justice, the human dignity of all people, and the liberation of the oppressed. God's unconditional and everlasting love for *all* human beings presupposes love in human relationship for all who enter into covenant with this God. Love in human relationships presupposes a commitment to justice, dignity, and wholeness in the structures or systems of society.

As I've familiarized myself with the biblical tradition, reading it over and over, studying it, and reflecting on it, the point that keeps coming forth is how often God's love or grace is a disturbing one. God's love or mercy functions as a disturbing influence and power in the lives of the people. In fact whenever God shows up, there is frequently a disturbance of the peace of some kind. And God has a way of showing up just about everywhere.

The God of the Bible is the One who invades and intrudes. The late Rabbi Abraham Heschel used to say that the function of the prophets was interference. In the initial biblical story involving created beings, God appears as a Disturbing Question in the midst of the human situation (the place: the garden; the cast: the woman, the man, the serpent, and God). The disturbing inquiry is met with evasions by both the man and the woman. They hide from the Radical Questioner and use the two best-known rationalizations for their evasiveness—to blame another person and to blame the circumstances or situations of life in which we find ourselves.

This scene, on page 3 of my Revised Standard Version, sets the tone for the 994 Old Testament pages that follow. The entire Exodus episode is the story of divine disturbance. God interferes with Moses' tranquil flock-tending on the west side of the wilderness. The burning bush is the sign of holy disturbance, of the invasion taking place. Mind you, Moses was minding his own business. The Disturbing One has a job for Moses: "I have seen the affliction of my people who are in Egypt, and have heard their cry. . . . I have come down to deliver them. . . . Come, I will send you to Pharaoh that you may bring forth my people" (Exod. 3). By this time Moses is thinking that either he has lost his mind or that God has. Answer: "Who am I that I should go to Pharaoh. . . . They will not believe me. . . . I am not eloquent. . . . Send, I pray, some other person . . ." (Exod. 3 and 4). The Disturbing One will not be denied. Aaron is enlisted along with Moses, and the disturbing mission is launched.

Pharaoh is next in the plan of disturbance. The intensity of his disturbance is clearly revealed in the number and assortment of plagues he is willing to endure in order to sustain his system of oppression. Blood. Frogs. Gnats. Flies. Boils. Hail. Locusts. Darkness. Death of the First-born. Loss of political power and prestige, loss of a plentiful supply of cheap labor, and thus loss of an economic system benefiting the aristocracy: these are the losses that oppressors resist at virtually any cost. Obviously this is not merely ancient history. South Africa, Rhodesia, North and South Korea, the Soviet Union, the military dictatorships of Latin America, and the suppression of fundamental human rights of the farm workers of America are ample testimonies to the hardness of heart that enslaves oppressors in their oppression of others. The long history of injustices toward Native Americans, women, and ethnics has been previously lifted up in Chapter One.

Even the Israelite people are disturbed in God's act of deliverance. Their dependable routine in bondage, their servile security, and their protection from the ambiguity implied in freedom of choice are disturbed as they are liberated for a new future. In the wilderness they murmur and complain. "Would that we had died by the hand of the Lord in the land of Egypt, when we sat by the fleshpots and ate bread to the full; for you have brought us out into this wilderness to kill this whole assembly with hunger" (Exod. 16:3). The Good News of liberation will seem like Bad News at times even to those who are being liberated!

As for Pharaoh, the Good News of liberation for the People of Israel was Bad News for his system of domination. If there is Good News for the oppressed it has to be Bad News for the system of the oppressor. It cannot be both ways. If the Good News that is Bad News breaks through a hardness of heart and occasions repentance, the Good News for the weak that comes as Bad News for the strong then becomes Good News for all. As long as Pharaoh insists on a system of imposed suffering or oppression of others, the Good News to Israel will be Bad News to Pharaoh. But if Pharaoh comes to value the rights of others above exploitative gain, the Exodus will become his Good News, too. He is no longer dependent on the servitude of others for his identity and sense of meaning. He sees that this oppression of others is a denial of his own personhood as a human being. Whether or not the news is Good or Bad depends on "where we are" and "who we are" in relation to the news content.

The biblical revelation of God is one in which God comes again and again as a disturbing factor in the human picture—sometimes from burning bushes, sometimes from whirlwinds, and at other times from pillars of fire. The procession of prophets is often a story of interference and interruption of injustices perpetrated by the strong on the weak. The prophets in various ways and through diverse styles call Israel again and again to renewed faithfulness to the covenant with the God of justice, condemning oppression and uplifting the vision of a restored community.

Disturbance is a familiar pattern throughout the New Testament. In the tradition of the church Jesus has frequently been pictured as the Great Physician. I believe careful reflection will suggest that Jesus is often more like a surgeon than a general practitioner. Like a surgeon with a scalpel he seeks to disturb and cut away the diseased parts of our lives in order to bring healing. As in the Old Testament, the divine disturbance is an important part of the tradition, a dimension we are wont to neglect. It is more comfortable to focus on the friendly Good Shepherd than on the Jesus who drove out the temple moneychangers with a whip. We are more prone to center on the Jesus who calms the troubled seas than on the story of the man ill for thirty-eight years whose healing depended on entering the pool "when the water is troubled" (John 5).

My intention is not to suggest that we replace the stories of comfort and consolation with those that emphasize disturbance. My point is that our human condition will invariably lead us, through our own choices, to prefer those narratives that comfort our affliction over those that afflict our comfort. If we do this consistently—and I *know* this is my inevitable tendency for myself—we begin to remake the gospel in our own image. Before long we are shaping the gospel so that it looks like us and sounds like us. And that of course means the gospel has no power to change us because all it does is confirm where we already are. In Christian theology the name given to this practice is idolatry.

The gospel of Mark particularly emphasizes the conflict surrounding Jesus' ministry. I have long been convinced that the story of the Gerasene demoniac (Mark 5:1-20) is one of the most profound passages in Scripture. Never before have I attempted to put some of its treasures in writing, although I have preached from it on numerous occasions. The first several verses of this text will occupy our attention now.

They came to the other side of the sea, to the country of the Gerasenes. And when he had come out of the boat, there met him out of the tombs a man with an unclean spirit, who lived among the tombs; and no one could bind him anymore, even with a chain; for he had often been bound with fetters and chains, but the chains he wrenched apart, and the fetters he broke in pieces; and no one had the strength to subdue him. Night and day among the tombs and on the mountains he was always crying out, and bruising himself with stones. And when he saw Jesus from afar, he ran and worshipped him; and crying out with a loud voice, he said, "What have you to do with me, Jesus, Son of the Most High God? I adjure you by God, do not torment me." For he had said to him, "Come out of the man, you unclean spirit!" And Jesus asked him, "What is your name?" He replied, "My name is Legion; for we are many." And he begged him eagerly not to send them out of the country. Now a great herd of swine was feeding there on the hillside; and they begged him, "Send us to the swine, let us enter them." So he gave them leave. And the unclean spirits came out, and entered the swine; and the herd, numbering about two thousand, rushed down the steep bank into the sea, and were drowned in the sea.

The herdsmen fled, and told it in the city and in the country. And people came to see what it was that had happened. And they came to Jesus, and saw the demoniac sitting there, clothed and in his right mind, the man who had had the legion; and they were afraid. And those who had seen it told what had happened to the demoniac and to the swine. And they began to beg Jesus to depart from their neighborhood. And as he was getting into the boat, the man who had been possessed with demons begged him that he might be with him. But he refused, and said to him, "Go home to your friends, and tell them how much the Lord has done for you, and how he has had mercy on you." And he went away and began to proclaim in the Decapolis how much Jesus had done for him; and all men marveled.

The story is superb drama from start to finish. As usual, Jesus is initiating movement toward the people. When he sets foot on the shore, he is met by a man who lives among the tombs, who has an unclean spirit, and who is always crying out and bruising himself. At first glance this might sound to some like a scene from the back ward of a mental hospital. With imagination—a requisite for getting inside first century thought forms—we see instead a microcosm of the world as it is today. The composite picture includes the isolation and alienation of our lives, both external and within the self. We might think of it as living among the tombs. Not much creative reflection is required to recount the endless ways in which human beings are always crying out for meaning, for a sense of purpose, for a coherent identity. And who among us is not at times our own worst enemy, bruising ourselves "with stones" as it were. The Gerasene demoniac is a collective and yet individualized picture of us all. He is in us. We are in him. We are fractured, bruised, and frenetic humanity.

The encounter of the demoniac with the one who delivers is memorable. He runs toward Jesus to worship him and exclaims, "What have you to do with me, Jesus, Son of the Most High God? I adjure you by God, do not torment me." But these are not the first words of the encounter. The first words have already been spoken, although that fact is not revealed until the next verse following the demoniac's plea. For Jesus, we are told, had *already* said to him, "Come out of the man, you unclean spirit!" (v. 8).

Whatever the man's agony, his distress did not keep him from seeing clearly that involvement with Jesus would mean disturbance. The response is an accurate portrayal of the divine-human encounter. The ambience of the encounter is ambivalence. We want to worship, yet we do not want to be disturbed. We have grown accustomed to our demons and thus dependent on them. Don't send them too far away, Lord! We are compelled, yet repelled; attracted, yet repulsed. You remember the old saying: "Lord, save us, but not now. Later on." That's the way we are. "Lord, take away my self-pity. I don't need that anymore. Lord, something in me gets some mileage from my self-pity. Leave it be. Lord, cast out my lovelessness and free me to care. Lord, it's too scary and risky to love. Leave me as I am. Lord, come toward me so I can commit myself to you. Lord, don't get too close. It's too threatening."

I believe this passage profoundly describes our relationship to God. We want the Good News of the gospel but we do not want it to disturb us. The fact of a disturbing grace is firmly rooted in Scripture. No picture of Jesus is biblically complete unless it includes Jesus the Tormentor, the bearer of God's disturbing love. He torments our torment, both realized and unrealized. He disturbs our illusions with the truth in order to make us free. He torments our greed with the gospel of solidarity with others. He challenges our lovelessness with a life of risk and outreach. He calls into question our idolatry of despair with a message of hope. To neglect this dimension of our biblical heritage is to render the gospel trivial and insipid.

Autobiographical Disturbance

Sometimes I say to a congregation, "If I were to ask you to share with each other how the gospel has disturbed you through the years from time to time, what would that sound like?" I expect the outcome would be fascinating. We would hear some absorbing storytelling about great changes in human life. Perhaps some would not be able to recall a single instance of significant disturbance. Where would you come out? If you draw a blank on that, could it mean that what we call Christian disciple-ship is no more than our cultural norms warmed over with a few pious phrases, images, and quotes? How have you been transformed instead of conformed to our world?

As I get in touch with my own years, I realize that it took me a long time to come to one of the major discoveries of my life: namely, that *God loves me enough to disturb me.* God's tormenting grace is a sign of liberating love. God is a critical lover! This realization from biblical history can open a person to new possibilities for life, many of which are painful before they are promising and fulfilling. For me the gospel has been like a Roto-Rooter, churning through my resistances and turning my presuppositions and priorities upside down.

All my life, from time to time, I've sung "Blessed Assurance, Jesus is Mine." These words can become little more than a sentimental exercise in reducing Jesus to our own size unless accompanied by the theme, "Blessed Disturbance, I am Christ's!" Not that I welcome God's distur-bance when it occurs in the midst of my life. At least, though, I've learned from past experience that sometimes the news I thought was Bad News turned out to be some of the Best News I'd ever heard. If and when I can draw on this personal experience of the past, it means that I can be open to the disturbing love which is presently confronting me.

I wish I couldn't, but I can remember all too clearly in 1950 a position I took as an undergraduate regarding the racial clause in my fraternity's constitution. Across the country there raged a debate about fraternity policies and practices. My fraternity's constitution limited members "to those of the Aryan race," or some such words. "The fraternity will be lost in the South," I now painfully recall debating at our chapter meeting. That's who I was at the midpoint of the century. My parents did not consciously teach me racism. I absorbed it by "cultural osmosis," that is, the attitudes of my society were adopted unconsciously as my own.

When I look back on those days now, I do so in disbelief. Not long afterwards I came under the influence of another understanding of humanity. At first the universal or global concept of humanity that we call Christian sounded like Bad News. I wanted no part of it. My initial response was, "Get away from me and leave me alone. Do not torment me." My demons resisted being sent away! The word of equality contradicted the cultural standards that had been my standards. Thank God that God loved me enough to disturb me! As I begin to receive the disturbance and as I begin to experience its truth, the Word that sounded like Bad News became Good News. What seemed like judgment turned into mercy. The Blessed Disturbance brought about the death of my narrow, smug provincialism, and the birth of a joyous discovery of a new concept of brotherhood and sisterhood. Experiences like this have convinced me that the Blessed Disturbance hurts too much—and heals too much—to be anything else but God's Word.

Thank God, the gospel has interfered with my life in countless ways. When I have sought security, the gospel has pointed to loving risk for others. When my vested interests have blinded me, the gospel has beckoned me to open my eyes to the world beyond my own interests. When I get hooked on status and prestige, the gospel holds before me the picture of a crucified Savior. When I begin to think that my personal attitudes and acts are all that count, the gospel reminds me of my participation in powers and principalities, in systems and structures that by their very existence contribute to my advantage and to the dehumanizing disadvantage of others. The Roto-Rooter churns through the channels of my spirit, clearing and cleansing the impediments that clog up the life of faith. The autobiography of any Christian must surely be incomplete apart from the disturbing probings and promptings of the Christian gospel at the core of our lives, just as the story of our lives is likewise the story of God's promise of boundless and everlasting love for each of us. In fact God's disturbing love cannot be distinguished from that boundless and everlasting love in which we live and die and have our being.

In recent months I have become increasingly aware that God not only disturbs me as an act of love for my liberation; God's love will also disturb me as others experience their liberation. A recent event in my life symbolized this for me. I was in a hurry on an extremely cold December day to reach the Kansas City International Airport to meet a friend. As I neared the Paseo bridge, a huge traffic tie-up developed and soon I found myself in bumper-to-bumper traffic. Time began to slip away and I still had a long way to go to reach the airport on time. I fussed, fumed, and fretted. What on earth was causing the problem, and why did it have to happen to me at this time?

As my traffic line inched its way onto the bridge itself, seven or eight police cars came into view along with several cars of local T.V. stations. An accident? A homicide? There was no sign of a wreck and it remained a mystery as to the cause of the problem. As it turned out, the inconvenience was over soon enough for me to barely make my friend's incoming flight on time. The incident was forgotten.

Until I picked up the paper the next morning. The front page headline, pictures, and article recounted a dramatic episode on the underside of the bridge. Answering a report that a young man was apparently poised to jump to an almost certain death in the icy waters of the Missouri River below, a policeman had positioned himself below the bridge a few feet from the man. With help from colleagues on the bridge, the policeman harnessed himself in a rope and precariously moved toward the man on a narrow ledge. About the time it appeared to the policeman that he might convince the man not to jump, the man leaped off the ledge.

At precisely the critical moment the policeman also leaped and caught the man in mid-air, both being supported by the policeman's rope harness from the top side of the bridge. There they dangled and struggled with each other. The policeman told the struggling man, "I'm going to hold on to you till hell freezes over, and if you go down, I go down with you." Following agonizing moments of uncertain maneuvering, they were both pulled to safety. One man had risked his life. Another man's life was saved.

As I read the story, I realized that all I had seen was my own inconvenience. A dramatic rescue was taking place. The meaning of the Incarnation was being acted out almost under my nose. Like the Gerasene demoniac, the man who was poised to jump to destruction is in all of us. We, too, are again and again poised to jump into our illusions, into despair and self-negation, into rejection of life. In addition the event reminded me that when dominated groups—whether Third World people, women, or ethnic minorities—come into their rightful place of dignity and power, the rest of us will experience inconvenience, interruption, interference. Since we have benefited from privileged systems that have denied others a decent life—such as subhuman living conditions of U.S. farm workers who have made products available for our tables—the amendment, alteration, or abolishment of these systems will interfere with the privileges we have desired and thus bring an end to our illusions.

> When the oppressed affirm their freedom by refusing to behave according to the master's rules, they not only liberate themselves from oppression, but they also liberate the oppressors from an enslavement to their illusions.[1]

Due to the world neighborhood in which we all now live, I am learning to *expect* that the liberation of others will interfere with the advantages I have known from the status quo. More importantly, as I experience my identity in Jesus Christ, the seeming interferences from the liberation of others are in reality calling me to a deeper humanity. The vision of a new humanity is the affirmation that justice and dignity for all is more important than privilege and prosperity for a few.

The Church in Need of Divine Disturbance

To be in touch with the biblical heritage is to *expect* to be disturbed by the Holy One of Israel, by the living Lord of History. To enter into the covenant by baptism, and to ratify that entrance through confirmation, is to *expect* inquiry, inconvenience, interference. This expectation is one of the distinguishing marks of the Christian community, or at least it should be. I'm speaking of a disturbance that is firmly rooted in sound biblical theology and in careful secular homework and fact finding. I'm speaking of a disturbance whose wellspring is the desire to speak the truth in love. Too often the church is disturbed for the wrong reasons: ministers whose self-rejection is projected onto others; trivial institutional matters that are insignificant to the church's mission in the world; church members who want all comfort and no challenge.

In the past year I've come to realize that the church is the *only* community or organization to which I belong *precisely in order to be disturbed.* Not that a well thought out disturbance grounded in biblical theology is the *only* reason I belong! But Christianly speaking I know that I'm not getting what I should unless the ministry of the church—the preaching, the education, the fellowship, and the mission in the world— prompt me to re-evaluate who I am, why I am, and where I am. I do not expect civic organizations and clubs to perform this function, at least not in an intentional manner intrinsic to their reason for existence.

When the disturbance function does not occur, I know that I'm the loser. A sound Christian theology has a prominent place for the doctrine of original sin. This doctrine essentially means that all of us have an inevitable tendency to look after our own interest to the detriment of others and that we need all the help we can get in struggling with this tendency to make ourselves the all in all of the universe. When we *expect* the church to disturb us at this point, and when we expect our support of the church to help bring this about for ourselves and for others, we have, so to speak, turned a corner as Christians, and are beginning to think like *biblical* Christians.

Recently I met a United Methodist layman from Little Rock who told me he was upset with his minister. When asked why, he replied, "He never preaches anything that can upset anyone. He is scared to death of anything close to boat-rocking. He talks about love but always in the most general platitudes. There's no challenge anymore for me in church." May God increase his tribe!

Unfortunately, the majority of Christians apparently want the church to be a comfort station rather than a community of challenge. As long as most Christians expect the Cross to be a decorative design in the sanctuary instead of a sign and seal of discipleship, the church's life and mission will be merely a domesticated religion of benign spirituality. Without Divine Disturbance, the church becomes a haven for pious platitudes, placebos, and palliatives.

Following a speech in Kansas City, former CBS correspondent Daniel Schorr was asked if he thought that what is released to the U.S. public should be related to what the public can receive, insofar as the latter is measurable. He replied that the information you don't want may be more important than the information you do want. If you merely give the people what they want, then you just have a happy hour.

My fear for the Christian church is that our common worship and our life together will degenerate into little more than a happy hour. We are continually tempted to say, "Speak to us smooth things, prophesy illusions, let us hear no more of the Holy One of Israel" (Isa. 30). Let us have a happy hour of harmony and tranquility. Bonhoeffer reminded us that cheap grace is the deadly enemy of the church, and that the church must fight for costly grace. If the preached and taught Word of God does not call for amendment of life as a response to God's grace, then either some are not getting their money's worth or we have tuned out the God who loves us enough to disturb us, whose disturbing Word is in fact our profoundest hope.

The Disturbance of Liberation Theology

In the Appendix some of the theological criticisms that are sometimes directed at liberation theologies are explored. One can have some reservations about the theological adequacy or method of liberation theologies, yet affirm the essential rightness of their imperatives for the church and the world. The deeper issue is the personal one of "Where do I stand in relation to the claims of liberation theologies?" "What is my response?" Before we can examine our own response to liberation theologies, and/or a view of Liberation Theology for the Privileged and the Prosperous (Chapters Four through Seven), we will do well to be mindful of some of our personal resistances. I'm going to reflect on two of my own resistances which I believe to be fairly typical of the privileged and the prosperous.[2]

The first resistance for most of us in the affluent sector of society is the difficulty of perceiving ourselves as oppressors. We go about our daily work, raise our families, support the church and/or various civic organizations that reach out to human need, enjoy a few friends, and live out our lives. So what's so oppressive about that? Brown voices the position of many of us, "It's not my fault that other people are oppressed. I don't have enough power to oppress anybody, and what's more, I don't have enough power to stop those with power from acting oppressively."[3]

My quarrel with my own resistance is twofold. The first is to expose myself to a growing awareness of the individual influence that I do have. I do have a vote. I have opportunities to express opinions to others. I can join with others in order to bring changes in city, county, or state governments as they impact the lives of ethnic minorities and women in this country. To the extent that I do not take these opportunities seriously, I am part of the problem instead of part of the possible solution, and thus am an unintentional oppressor through indifference and default of my responsibilities. Although my individual responsibility may be a mere "drop in the bucket" when seen in relation to the whole, that "drop in the bucket" is all important to the meaning of my life as well as to the network of other responses around me.

The hardest truth to hear, however, is that even if I do take the above responsibilities seriously, I am still part of an oppressive system that takes away from others. We have learned to think so individualistically that our grasp of systemic issues is not easily achieved. If it is true that I have more goods to choose from because laborers in Latin America have been exploited through American corporations and United States government policies, I am part of an oppressive system and in that sense I am an oppressor in a corporate, systemic way. I may feel almost helpless to change "what is" in terms of the system, but I am still part of that system that takes from others, and thereby involved. "No argument that totally disengages us from the actions of our nation is finally defensible."[4]

If my identity is truly in Jesus Christ, I need not become defensive about the fact that in some ways I am an oppressor in individual relationships . . . and that I am also involved in a web of institutional or corporate forms of racism, sexism, and nationalistic aggrandizement. In Jesus Christ I need only to try to understand the fact of oppression, my involvement in it, and how liberation of others and of myself can become the script of my life. This will never be easy or comfortable, but in Jesus Christ there will be neither complacency nor despair.

A second resistance has to do with what Rosemary Ruether has called a "sense of just proportions" in relation to oppression.[5] There is a sense in which everyone is oppressed in some way. This can be used to dull one's sensitivity to the distinctions between degrees of oppression. When this happens to us, we lose our sensitivity to the desperate situations that surround the lives of so many human beings. While our own problems may seem oppressive, who among us, especially white males, would willingly trade our "oppression" for daily hunger or malnutrition, for indecent housing and rampant disease, for the tyranny of military dictatorships and absence of civil liberties? What I discover is that most of my own problems—like the "oppression" of inflation in financing a theological seminary with a very tiny endowment—are sometimes placed in a more holistic perspective when I consider the level of oppression of so many others in the world. When I remember that the majority of the world's people do not know for sure whether their next meal will be forthcoming, it does put a different light on how I go about trying to cope with my particular problems.

For those of us in the privileged and the prosperous segment of society, the crux of the matter is not finally our theological analysis of liberation theologies, although we need to do our homework in that respect. To get hung up in theological analysis is to repeat some mistakes already made. That is, during the 1960s the affluent white community authorized many studies and reports on the inner cities and the minority communities. After a few years of "expertism" on what was wrong with others, it began to be understood that the research needed to center on those doing the research and on the centers of power that they represented.

The same is true now in the discipline of theology. We all need to form our opinions about the content and methods of liberation theology. Most of all, however, we need to turn our questions inward with inquiries like these: What are the implications of liberation theologies for my lifestyle? For the system in which I live? If we construct a liberation theology for the privileged and the prosperous, where would the contours come from and go to? Can we develop a theology of liberation that draws on the life situation of the oppressor, as existing liberation theologies draw on the life situation of the oppressed?

Hoping that this chapter has helped to open a door to God's disturbing love, we are ready now to work on the above questions in the chapter that follows. In dealing with these questions we are directly involved in the process of resistance and response to liberation theology. If liberation theologies proclaim costly grace to us all, and I believe that they do, we must in turn speak of responsibility. For where there is grace there is responsibility.

CHAPTER FOUR

The Good Life Redefined:
Abrahamic/Zacchaean Lifestyles

In the previous chapter I laid the foundation for liberation theology in a fourth dimension. We have considered the concept of critical love as a distinctive biblical perspective, and I have suggested that our most profound hope lies in God's disturbing love that will not leave us alone. We have in previous chapters attempted to listen to the broad outlines of feminist, black, and Third World theologies. This chapter will be pointing to several contours and implications of a liberation theology and ethic for privileged and prosperous Christians.

Translating Liberation Theology into Our Own Situation

Can a theology for the oppressed become a theology for the privileged and the prosperous? If we put the question this way, the answer must be negative. Our histories are almost total opposites, and the experiences today of haves and have-nots are radically different. Theology is always contextual and proceeds from an environment containing various presuppositions. Therefore one cannot simply transfer or superimpose one on the other.

However, I do believe that existing theologies of liberation can provide *directions for* a theology pertinent to the privileged and prosperous. In fact I would want to insist that theology "for the rest of us" can be authentically and adequately shaped *only in relation to* and *in response* to black, Third World, and feminist theologies.

The search for a usable past has become an integral part of liberation theologies. It is worth noting that at the very time liberation theologies are

47

pointing to the discovery of heroes and heroines from the past, the affluent white male community is recognizing how sordid much of our past history has been, and what's more, how tarnished so many of our heroes have become. Many theologians of the past were blinded by the cultural norms of the day, and thus did not question male primacy. Neither did their theological systems make a major place for addressing the deprivation of ethnic minorities or Third World people.

When we look at the history of western civilization, we don't have to look very long to discern a customary low regard for women, the enslavement of African people for economic gain, the neocolonialization of Latin American countries, and the winning of the West through genocide against Native Americans. All of this by a people who by and large thought of themselves as Christians! What does this unenviable record mean to us today?

It means that our first step is to take seriously the New Testament Good News that "no human being can boast in the presence of God because God is the source of your life in Christ Jesus, whom God made our wisdom, our righteousness and sanctification and redemption" (1 Cor. 1:29-30). Only from this point of view can we be freed from the need for excuses, rationalizations, defensive maneuvers, and unnecessary paralyzing guilt. When Jesus Christ is our justification, we can welcome the human gifts of all persons and groups as complementary instead of competitive, as contributive to total human well-being instead of as threats to our security and status. We are neither condemned nor justified by what has or has not happened in the past. Our future is given and made open only by the re-creative gift of God.

A second point is that we need to understand our history and to acknowledge it as it has more fully come to light. If we deny what was, the future will be a replay of the past. To discover a usable past we must accept the factual reality of the past and at the same time reject its features of oppression. This denunciation should amount to a commitment to help bring about a future that is radically different.

A third step toward combining a usable past with a transformed future is a selective process by which we combine faith exemplars from our own tradition with those of other cultures and races. The hall of heroes and heroines, so to speak, will need to be re-examined. Some of our hallowed ancestors will remain so even though their clay feet may be a bit more prominent in the light of a more inclusive revelation of history made known by liberation theologies. In addition the spectrum of saints will expand as we embrace ethnic minority, female, and Third World persons whose lives convey a fresh word to us, a word "for us" even as it may be "over against" us.

An impoverishment of exemplars to emulate has become a wide-spread phenomenon in our society. For example, "in a recent survey of 1200 junior high school students, the most popular response to the question, 'Who is your hero?,' was 'None' "[1] A society which has no humane models for the future will be incapable of nurturing a sense of that which deserves to be loved and appreciated, especially purposes which demand sacrifice, courage, and compassion beyond the im-mediate concerns of the self. Later in this chapter I will hold up a particular example that has grasped my attention in recent days.

Identity in Christ, an honest reckoning of the past, a recovering of an array of exemplars on a global basis both past and present—these are some of the prerequisites as we move in the direction of a new theology of liberation.

Costly Free Grace

I believe that the most important task for the church today, especially the church of the privileged and the prosperous, is the creative and audacious merger of free grace and costly grace. The Christian gospel is a combination of free grace that is not cheap, and costly grace that is not works righteousness but an unmerited gift. Free grace that is received as gift apart from demand is an offense to the crucified messiah, a sentimen-tal testimony to "sloppy agape." Costly grace that is claim without promise becomes an unbearable burden that leads to despair or self-righteousness.

In one of Charles Schulz's Peanuts cartoons, Linus is reading a note from his mother as he prepares to eat his sack lunch at school. The note reads as follows: "Dear Son, I hope you enjoy and also appreciate the lunch I made for you today. Did you have a nice morning? Did you volunteer in class as I suggested? Teachers are always impressed by students who volunteer. It is a sure way to better grades. Remember, better grades now will mean a better college later on. Did you eat your carrots? Proper nutrition is essential to good study. Are you sitting in the sun? I hope so, for a little sun is good as long as we don't overdo it. Perhaps ten minutes a day this time of year is about right."

At this point Charlie Brown walks up to Linus, saying, "Hi, Linus. What are you having for lunch?" Linus answers, "Carrots, peanut butter, and guilt!"[2]

Any effort to proclaim the gospel, live it, or even write about it is carrots, peanut butter, and guilt apart from the Good News of God's uncondi-tional, unmerited love. We are loved not because of what we do but because we are God's own. Christ died for the ungodly while we were yet sinners. To acknowledge God's love is to affirm that it is given to all other human beings just as it is offered to me.

But God's free grace or unconditional love is a costly grace. It is costly because to be grasped by this grace is "to yield ourselves to God as those who have been brought from death to life" (Rom. 6:13). The old life dies and a new creature is born in the likeness of Christ, the One who "emptied himself, taking the form of a servant" (Phil. 2:7). God's free grace re-forms and reshapes our lives in the mind and spirit of Christ, the Crucified/Risen One. Uncostly free grace is a cheap Easter, and thus without profound joy, power, and comfort. An earned costly grace is an unredeemable Bad Friday, an invitation to the hardness of heart or self-boasting of legalism.

The unity of costly free grace was visually dramatized for me on an Easter Sunday at the Dumbarton United Methodist Church in the Washington, D.C., area. On the preceding Good Friday evening my family and I had attended the congregation's Tenebrae Service. The liturgy, involving drama and action, was prepared and acted out by members of the congregation. When the service concluded, there was total darkness surrounding the people and a large black shroud draped over a free standing cross.

The Easter morning service, as well as the Tenebrae drama, was enlivened by a member of the congregation whose role was that of a clown. Dressed for the part, she distributed flowers and at unexpected points in the service utilized mime and motion. Just as the preacher stood and began his Easter sermon, the clown quietly went to the cross, deftly lifted the Tenebrae shroud from it, and approached the astonished preacher face to face, lifting the shroud over his head and draping it around his shoulders as an Easter stole!

Liberation theology for the privileged and prosperous is firmly rooted in God's free grace or unconditional love, which always beckons us to "faith working through love" as an expression of our thankful appropriation. The radical indicative—God's unmerited love—has been lifted up too often by the church apart from the radical imperative—God's mission in the world, which is empowered by and presupposed in the radical indicative. The late Rabbi Abraham Heschel got to the heart of the matter in saying that we tend to go through life asking the wrong questions. We ask, "How can I be saved?" Heschel said that to take God seriously is to ask, "How can I join God in the world and be about God's task?"

Liberation theology for privileged and prosperous Christians is not carrots, peanut butter, and guilt. We can experience a redefinition of the Good Life through the costly free grace of a God who loves us enough to disturb us.

Jesus Christ and the Good Life

Liberation theology becomes translated for privileged and prosperous Christians when it calls us to move *toward* the suffering and the power-lessness of the world's majority in our decisions and lifestyles. As we move toward human suffering, we will be moving toward the point of departure for existing liberation theologies. Privileged and prosperous Christians who decide in favor of moving toward the suffering of the world will experience a closer and deeper relationship with Jesus Christ, even as that relationship is already the propelling and impelling force behind the decision itself. Jesus Christ becomes our justification, our wisdom, and our sanctification, not just in verbal formulas, but in reality.

In the previous chapter the Mark 5 account of the Gerasene demoniac was a touchstone through which we reflected on the fact that God loves us enough to disturb us. If we continue in that passage, we find that God's disturbing love is a healing love. "And they came to Jesus, and saw the demoniac sitting there, clothed and in his right mind, the man who had had the legion" (v. 15).

Who are you when you are in your right mind? Who am I, and what am I like when I'm not in my right mind? "Mind" in this passage means more than the intellect or the cognitive function. It means the self, the whole person. Who are we when we are, so to speak, our real, authentic, genuine selves whom God created us to be and become? We might even ask it this way: Who are we when we are our "Jesus Christ" selves, that is, the self which somehow is open to and reliant on God's grace for the future?

When I'm not in my right mind, my definition of the Good Life becomes centered on acquisitiveness, personal security, competition for rank and position, and creating as much distance as possible between myself and the hurts of the world. The Good Life becomes a life of conformity, absence of commitment to great human causes, and insula-tion from a global vision of history and humanity.

When I'm in my right mind through Jesus Christ, my view of the Good Life is turned upside down. The other view then seems like a formula for boredom, selfishness, and withdrawal. More like an opiate, the demonic view of the Good Life dulls the senses, shrivels the depth of vision, and reduces life to measurements of competition and material possessions. It is its own brand of impoverishment. There is no lower standard of living than indifference amidst plenty. There is nothing more imprisoning than to be locked into a wrong idea. In reflecting on the massive suffering in today's world, Mary Buckley exclaims in *Liberation, Revolution, and*

Freedom, "Gradually I recognize that I cannot live in peace in the midst of such injustice; my own luxury turns against me and makes life meaningless."[3]

Bonhoeffer's definition of a Christian is this: "It is not the religious act that makes the Christian, but participation in the sufferings of God in the secular life,"[4] or paraphrased, "It is not some religious act which makes a Christian what she or he is, but participation in the suffering of God in the life of the world." Sometimes I wish I had never heard that definition because I'm more likely to be putting as much distance as possible between myself and the cries of the downtrodden—until by the costly free grace of God I am once again delivered into my right mind. Then I realize all over again that moving beyond my own vested interests for the sake of others is what it means to be a *human* being. As the man said who was lifting heavy boxes of goods and supplies that had been collected for victims of a storm, "It hurts good!"

In the Gerasene demoniac text, the response of the neighborhood to a man now in his right mind is instructive (Mark 5:14-18). If I had been constructing this text, I could imagine that the neighborhood would call for a celebration, a "kill the fatted calf" sort of thing. This our brother was in bondage and is reconciled with himself. But Scripture penetrates into the inner citadel of human experience. It breaks open the hidden layers of the heart and soul.

Verse 15 tells us that the neighborhood response was fear. The drama is intense. In verse 17 the neighborhood is begging Jesus to leave. In verse 18 the man in his right mind is also begging Jesus—to be with him! What is there about people in their right mind that is a threat? Is it not that they expose the sham and hypocrisy in our system of power? Do they not unmask the double standards that are disguised as the accepted cultural mores? There is no occasion for smugness here. If we have never begged the Lord of Life to depart and leave us alone, it is surely because the gospel has been received as flabby grace. When we sniff out the Good News that sounds like Bad News from where we are at that moment, we are prone to exclaim, "Let us hear no more of the Holy One of Israel!" (Isa. 30:11).

We know that this text is recycled in every period of history. It is the story of the first Christians under Caesar. It is happening on every continent in the world today. Those who speak the voice of sanity are the vulnerable ones. The neighborhood often says, "Get out and depart from our midst!" Two church women in Ireland. The voice of the poet in the Soviet Union. Growing numbers of priests, ministers, and lay persons in virtually every Latin American nation.

Again, if I had been writing the text I might have thought that Jesus
would have responded affirmatively to the man's request to go with him.
Here we see the genius of the gospel. The words of the text are, "But
Jesus refused" (v. 19). Jesus says to the man, "Go home to your friends
and tell them how much the Lord had done for you, and how the Lord
has had mercy on you" (v. 19). The choreography of the gospel is
always, "Come unto me; go into the world. Come; go. Gathered; scattered. Indicative; imperative. Grace; works. Justification; sanctification."

It is as though Jesus were saying, "You can't sit forever at my feet
soaking up great religious experiences as though I were a guru. Get out of
the sanctuary, out of the revival, off the mountain top. Go back into the
ambiguities of decision and action. Go back to your job, your family, your
neighborhood. Go back to politics, economics, and encounters with a
world of people living among the tombs, always crying out, and bruising
themselves and others. Go back into a world where the masses often fear
those who are in their right mind." There is a P.S. between the lines: "Lo,
I am with you always, until the end of the age."

Jesus Christ frees us for God's world. Our freedom in Christ for the
world means that God takes the whole world away from us and then gives
it back to us, not as a god, but as a gift, not as an end, but as a means for
discipleship. The world is taken away as our possession and is returned to
us as the arena of decision for faith working through love. Our style of life
becomes the means by which we intersect Jesus Christ in the world and
join in the liberating and emancipating work of God.

Abrahamic/Zacchaean Lifestyles: Cornucopia Through Kenosis

The family of Abraham, Dom Helder Camara tells us in *The Desert Is
Fertile*, is that worldwide community of men and women who are born to
serve others.[5] Composed of all races, languages, religions, and
ideologies, the Abrahamic minority is that called-out segment of humanity who perceive the Good Life as outreaching love to others. They are
ready to bend and expend themselves to build a more just and human
world. The trademark of the daughters and sons of Abraham is anonymous heroism on behalf of others.

For Abrahamic minorities, setting out on the road is the Good Life.

Setting out is first of all getting out of ourself, . . . to stop revolving
round ourself as if we were the centre of everything, . . . refusing to
be ringed in by the problems of our own small world. However
important these may be, mankind is more important and our task is

to serve mankind. Setting out is . . . first and foremost opening ourselves to other people, trying to get to know them, going out to meet them.[6]

Abraham's story, summarized in Hebrews 11:8-10, is a saga in which *cornucopia is displaced by kenosis*. The Good Life is redefined so that life is poured into life instead of protected against life. In our society cornucopia is the horn of plenty, thus an overflowing fullness or abundance. In biblical terms kenosis denotes Jesus' humbling and emptying himself (". . . who though he was in the form of God, did not count equality with God a thing to be grasped, but emptied himself, taking the form of a servant; . . . he humbled himself and became obedient unto death, even death on a cross") (Phil. 2:6-8). In more general terms, kenosis means an emptying. The Abrahamic horn of plenty comes from an emptying of self for others rather than from the accumulation of goods. Thus abundance comes from an emptying. The place of security and dominance is traded in favor of a risk-filled future for others. Robert McAfee Brown puts it this way: "Our displacement may not be geographical, but it will surely be ideological, theological, political, economic, and social."[7]

In the New Testament the Zacchaeus narrative in Luke (19:1-10) provides some clues for the good life redefined. Zacchaeus is the only affluent person in the gospels, other than the possible exception of Joseph of Arimathea, who responded with an Abrahamic-like faith to Jesus. We are told that Zacchaeus is a rich tax collector of Jericho who received Jesus into his home. The thrust of the story is apparently the contrast between the surly and complaining attitude of the crowd and the joyful, accepting attitude and response of Zacchaeus.

Zacchaeus belonged to a despised class of tax collectors. He was therefore an *outsider*. As we have seen, many New Testament stories portray Jesus' association with the poor, beggars, and other "unacceptables." Here we see him befriending a *rich* outcast instead of a poor one. The tables are turned, so to speak, and the pious orthodox are scandalized.

The story makes a familiar point with those who are steeped in New Testament study: God's grace is extended to all. The outcast, whether poor or rich, may be on the fringe of society but not on the fringe of God's grace. By limiting God's grace toward others, we cut ourselves away from that grace and the forgiveness toward others stemming from God's grace. In Matthew 21 Jesus warns the chief priests and the elders that the tax collectors and the harlots will go into the kingdom of God before they will. Similarly in the Zacchaeus passage, Jesus is telling the crowd that the joyous response of a despised tax collector puts to shame those who have limited God's grace by consigning others (like tax collectors) to labels and stereotypes.

In this passage it is also the case that through Jesus Christ a rich tax collector redefined the Good Life. Why? Maybe it was because a lonely, locked-in human being, eager for relationship and purpose in life, saw his whole life audited to the quick. Zacchaeus, having so much in a material sense, realized that he had nothing. "Why does this wandering carpenter who has nothing have more than I? Why does he have freedom of spirit, joy in life, compassion and care for others, and a sense of security, amidst all manner of threat? Why?"

Zacchaeus had everything but the Good Life. He did not have the Good Life because he had found neither himself nor others. Zacchaeus had props and protections but not life. Jesus' invitation was more than a request for a dinner host. Jesus' invitation was a moment of truth in which Zacchaeus realized a self-acceptance based on Jesus' acceptance. Zacchaeus found himself because he had been found by Jesus Christ. To be found by this one is to find oneself in the Abrahamic community, the pilgrims and pioneers who let go of their props in order to be free for others.

In Jesus Christ Zacchaeus found more than himself. He found a new ambition. This new ambition, this good life re-defined, began when he received Jesus joyfully (v. 7). Grace freely given and freely received becomes costly grace: "Behold, Lord, the half of my goods I give to the poor, and if I have defrauded anyone of anything, I restore it fourfold" (v. 8). The new ambition is the reordering of Zacchaeus' priorities. He is on the Abrahamic road for others. It is not by coincidence that in the text Jesus says to Zacchaeus, "Today salvation has come to this house, since he also is *a son of Abraham*" (v. 9). Even if Luke's point is addressed to the murmuring crowd in order to proclaim God's unconditional and universal grace, what is said about Zacchaeus cannot be dismissed lightly.

What does this story mean for the prosperous and privileged Christian? It tells us that God's grace encompasses outsiders, including the affluent. It tells us that the Abrahamic style of faith and life has to do with a new kind of security in God's kingdom, a security based on trust and confidence in God and in God's covenant community; with divestiture of power and wealth on behalf of others; and with a risk-filled availability of self and resources to meet the future needs of others as they arise. *This* is the Good Life Redefined. It is liberation from bondage.

In our society we have become indoctrinated and programmed for a life of individualism instead of individuality shaped by and existing for community. Self-denial for others has become suspect as human potential movements emphasize personal fulfillment and self-actualization. Perhaps the church has too often used the cruciform language of the Bible as a rationale for servility and submissiveness. Perhaps terms like "sacrifice" and "service" have been used falsely to promote paternalistic control through either guilt or stereotyped images. But self-denial, freely and intentionally chosen on behalf of others in the mind and spirit of Jesus Christ, is the anvil upon which solidarity with the powerless and the poor comes to pass. And it is the gateway to a more profound and joyous communion with God through Jesus Christ.

Any definition of individual liberation or self-fulfillment—given the conditions of life for the world's majority—that is not moving toward identification with human suffering and deprivation is not fulfillment. Instead it is a narcissistic cop-out, a euphemism for "me first and you last." How, then, can the Abrahamic/Zacchaean lifestyle move toward rather than away from the hurts and wounds of the world? How can the new cornucopia become a kenosis?

The Fast That Becomes a Feast

The fifty-eighth chapter of Isaiah provides us a beginning point for the Good Life Redefined. After return from exile the people are without vision and the nation languishes in gloom. In the next chapter we are told that justice is turned back and that truth has fallen in the public squares. So it is that the people humble themselves with fasting, sackcloth, and ashes.

The Lord's response initiates a radical reinterpretation of the fast.

> Is not this the fast that I choose: to loose the bonds of wickedness, to undo the thongs of the yoke, to let the oppressed go free, and to break every yoke? Is it not to share your bread with the hungry and bring the homeless poor into your house? . . . Then shall your light break forth like the dawn, and your healing shall spring up speedily. . . . If you pour yourself out for the hungry and satisfy the desire of the afflicted, then shall your light rise in the darkness, and your gloom be as the noonday. . . . You shall raise up the foundations of many generations; you shall be called the repairer of the breach, the restorer of streets to dwell in (excerpts from vv. 1-12).

In our day we can barely appreciate this transformation of the fasting concept in the light of its previous development in Israelite tradition and practice. What we see in this text is a major re-imaging of the fast from a cultic act to a compassionate one; from an ascetic act to an ethical act of social justice; from self-abasement to self-giving. The emphasis shifts from the security of religious custom to solidarity with the outcast and the oppressed. Thus, in the Good Life Redefined the fast for others becomes our feast of life, and our true feast is found in the fast for others. As our fast becomes a feast, and vice versa, kenosis has become the new cornucopia. As Abraham Heschel has written, "We must be able to say no to ourselves in the name of a higher yes."[8]

What happened to Zacchaeus is that the flowering of affluence turned into a souring of affluence. Through Jesus Christ his eyes and ears were opened to the world around him. As in our society today, an affluence that is not profoundly influenced by the suffering and want in the world can only be described as obscene. The church in its corporate practices will do well to follow the Zacchaean connection, recognizing that God is the owner of all land, goods, and possessions. Likewise, affluent individual Christians who participate in the Good Life Redefined will share in the feast of Christ through an economic fasting for others. By economic fasting I mean an intentional divestiture of resources for causes that feed the hungry and that work for social justice and world peace.

I believe that all of us who are affluent Christians should re-examine our relationship to economics. The more affluent we are, the more God wants us to experience feasting through fasting. What excuse is there for not turning *everything* over $30,000 income per year (or $25,000 or $35,000) to the cause of Jesus Christ? Avoid legalism and name your own level as a disciplined commitment. Whatever we name will fall far short of the idea of voluntary poverty as an act of solidarity with the poor and at the same time a protest against poverty. Even if we decided to live "comfortably" while the world's majority lives in squalor and pain, affluent Christians could fast for others to the tune of millions of dollars worth of fasting and feasting. This economic fasting for humankind could be a clue for a total lifestyle that moves toward others.

Our dilemma runs deeper. The truth is that many affluent Christians worship the economic system rather than the One who is Lord of economics. Our real God is the bottom line. In that respect we eat the same pie as Marxists; we just divide it differently. They divide it collectively; we divide it individually. The point is that it is *economics* that defines where our real heart or soul is located, regardless of how we divide it. Try this test on yourself: compare your feelings when the Christian faith is attacked by an atheist or by a person of some other religion with your feelings when capitalism or free enterprise is attacked.

The results may tell us where our treasure is to be found: in the kingdom of God or in the kingdom of Capitalism. If the latter is the winner, we have placed ourselves with Marxists in asserting that the organizing principle and final determinant of human history is *economics*. There will be disagreement in dividing the pie. But there will be agreement that economics, by whatever system, is the object of our deepest faith.

When I get "back to the Bible" in my studies and reflections on economics, here is a very broad overview of what I see: The earth is the Lord's and all therein; Yahweh is Lord of economics and demands economic justice among the people; in the community of Jesus Christ the promised kingdom is partially experienced through mutual sharing and support, for example, widespread economic sharing in the Christian church in Jerusalem (Acts 2:43-47; 4:32-37), transformed economic relationships, which meant financial availability to others in need (Acts 4:32-35), and economic sharing through the church at Corinth, which apparently presupposed an economic equality among the worldwide people of God (2 Cor. 8:1-15, particularly vv. 13-14). For Paul the fellowship of Christians, especially as experienced in the Eucharist, was utterly incompatible with economic disparity within the total membership.[9]

In relation to our own time the biblical emphasis on economics under God and the resulting sharing through community implies the avoidance of extremes of wealth and poverty. Since those extremes are all around us, we need to encourage "a massive discipling process in the churches, so that individual Christians would start living more simple lifestyles. . . . Churches, likewise, would need to adopt more simple corporate lifestyles."[10] The Christ Episcopal Church in Charlotte, North Carolina, is one example. Instead of erecting a new activities building, the congregation raised over $200,000 for the hungry, distributed among twelve local, national, and international projects.

The architectural motto of the late Mees Van der Rowe was "less is more." The Abrahamic/Zacchaean lifestyle explores ways in which less for oneself can be translated into more for others. "Less is more" can become an exercise of spiritual discipline and formation and at the same time an ethical fast which results in more for others. The fast that becomes the feast of Christ is for the sake of the common redemption of all humankind. It is not charity in the liberal or reformist sense. It is the recognition of one humanity and one history under God and must properly be the prelude for new systems that feature people priorities (Chapter Five).

Another image of fasting and feasting with which I would like to see

Christians wrestle, especially Protestants, is a translation of monastic life into our own situations. Until recently I have tended to regard the monastic life as an escape from the crucible of world suffering. While I still have some issues with monasticism, the style of simplicity, sharing, and solidarity of the monastic movement commends itself to a society bent on individualistic acquisition, accumulation, and advancement. I would like to see an increasing number of Christians exploring the gifts of the monastic movement. In so doing we might learn to place greater value on community and each life within community. New ways of sharing would be revealed to us, thereby reducing demands and our dependence on things.

Earlier in this chapter I indicated that I would hold before us an exemplar of the Abrahamic/Zacchaean venture who has become especially significant for me. How did I matriculate through three years of seminary in the 1950s without getting to know John Woolman? Elton Trueblood has called Woolman, an eighteenth-century Quaker, one of the most influential Quakers who ever lived. To me that is saying a great deal. Woolman is a sure example of the "less is more" lifestyle. For him the true feast of life was his fast for others.

He pleaded for black freedom long before the antislavery movement became prominent in the colonies. He refused to pay war taxes in order to be faithful to his pacifist conscience. In order to avoid bondage to things and to identify with humanity, he sought to live on the simplest economic level possible. He nurtured his empathy by deliberately seeking out experiences that developed his sensitivity to individuals and to the needs of society. Accordingly, he intentionally travelled on foot in the South to identify with the slaves. To experience the life of crew members, he crossed the ocean in steerage rather than in a cabin. In solidarity with Native Americans, he exposed himself to hardships they suffered.

As he moved toward the misery of others, he thanked God for leading him to a lively awareness of the affliction of others. Woolman's life expressed an incarnational style, called out in love and experiencing the fullness of life in emptying himself for others. Just as Good News is Bad News is Good News, so free grace is costly grace is free grace. For as Albert Schweitzer poetically states, "He commands. And to those who obey Him, whether they be wise or simple, He will reveal Himself in the toils, the conflicts, and the sufferings which they shall pass through in His fellowship, and, as an ineffable mystery, they shall learn in their own experience Who He is."[11]

I would hope that images of less is more and the fast that becomes a feast are clues that can be applied imaginatively to our total lives. The

Abrahamic/Zacchaean venture is not merely a matter of giving a little more money or giving up meat once a week. For that matter it is not merely a matter of giving a lot more money. The Good Life Redefined is a liberation lens by which we perceive all of life through Jesus Christ in the historical context of human suffering, scarcity, and the convulsive shaking of long-held cultural assumptions.

The Good Life Redefined: Male Mystiques and Personhood

The feminist movement in the church is calling the church back to its own faith in which there is "neither male nor female" (Gal. 3:28). If the Body of Christ is to resemble the spirit and the style of the One whose name it bears, it will be deeply concerned about women as persons; about intrinsic identity rather than derivative existence; about wider ranges of options and maximum utilization of human resources; about problems of salary discrimination and closed professional opportunities; about role conditioning and imaging; about liberation from assumptions nurtured for centuries through a patriarchal mindset.

As presented by the four evangelists, both the ministry and the message of Jesus in relation to women are unambiguous: God's love is extended unconditionally to all without regard to race, sex, or status. Indeed, the message goes a step further, namely, that God's special concern is identified with the oppressed and those who are treated as less than persons.[12]

I believe that God is calling forth a new white male humanness as surely as a new black, a new brown, a new red, or a new female humanness is being called forth. The liberation thrust for white males will come through the presence of the other religious and cultural liberations, as well as from white male initiative itself. Here I want to suggest two dimensions of this phenomenon.

From Masculine Mystique to the New Male Humanness

The first focus of men's liberation is on the self-image of the white male. The "masculine mystique," while less publicized than the feminine counterpart, is just as prominent. It, too, is the result of a stereotyped cultural conditioning that pervades our society. The self-image of the masculine mystique is rooted in the myth of the rugged individual, the so-called self-made man.

If ever there were an absurd, self-contradictory term, it is the phrase "self-made." No man is so tough and self-contained that he had no parents, no dependency needs as an infant, no process of development! The man-with-the-mystique admits few needs, since needs are tell-tale signs of weakness. He is a competitive winner for whom it is a disgrace to lose, and for whom failure is worse than death. The mystique insists on a facade of herculean strength.

Second, this mystique fosters the notion that women are inferior objects, dependent, passive, and helpless without male dominance. Manliness is connected with conquest of females. There is hardly need to chronicle the long-standing and pervasive suppression of women in virtually every realm of life—political, vocational, educational, legal, and social. The masculine mystique has shored up its own ego and image by convincing itself that the way things are is the only way men and women *can* relate.

Still another self-image of the white male is the assumption that children are women's responsibility and do not essentially belong within the tough demands of the masculine sphere. Male and female roles are seen as preordained, so that the male is substantially cut off from personal care and nurture for his own children. The male then becomes a proxy parent. The female is imaged only as a homemaker and thereby becomes a proxy citizen of the world through her husband. The masculine mystique, then, is a potpourri of John Wayne, James Bond, and Father Knows Best!

Consider now the counter-image, the "new male." The new male humanness is not limited or boxed in by cultural definitions, but instead participates in the new model of the more fully human male. I submit that this new male humanness is not simply a sociological change, but is definitely related to the insistence of the gospel for an egalitarian value orientation.

Three images of the new male come to mind, all of which are inherent in the gospel. First, there is the male who is not dependent on second-class identity or citizenship for women. For just as women have been excessively dependent on men for their identity, men have been excessively dependent on women with excessive dependency needs. How ironical that the mystique of the "self-made" male has been so dependent on dependent women! The new male thrives on equality of relationship and expects women to shed their submissive role, which dehumanizes both sexes.

Second, and closely connected with the first, I see a male who welcomes the growth and development of all other human beings—women, black men, brown men, red men. He welcomes their gifts to life and to society, believing that when a large percentage of the human race cannot give their gifts, then all humanity is stunted and dwarfed. He welcomes equality of human worth and of human opportunity, believing the gifts of others to society are fundamentally complementary rather than competitive, an enrichment rather than a diminution of his own selfhood.

Third, for the new male there is no prior definition of human traits as exclusively male or female. Cultural stereotypes have been reinforced from one generation to another, cutting off both male and female from a significant portion of our humanness. Men can be tender, gentle, empathic, and nurturing. Women can be practical, aggressive, effective, and self-confident. The question is not whether a certain trait is masculine or feminine by somebody else's absurd definition. The relevant questions are: What do you feel? What can you do? Why settle for half your humanness? Who says little boys must not cry? Who says little girls must be weak and dependent?

Need it even be said that the exodus from the old masculine mystique to the new male will come to us as both threat and promise? Let no one underestimate the repercussions of these changes. We do not wake up one morning and find ourselves transformed into the new male, already in the Promised Land. When an individual achieves a major change in personality or role functioning, it causes repercussions to every significant relationship experienced by that person. Family, friends, and associates must all make some sort of change in themselves in order to adapt.

Images of the New Male Humanness in Marriage

The second focus of men's liberation begins with the marriage of the masculine mystique to the feminine mystique. She needs to be dependent and he needs a dependent. The unwritten "contract" goes something like this: the wife will be the satellite or accessory with her identity gained through her husband instead of through herself. She will be known by his name, his reputation, and his sphere of influence. He will be the sun around which satellite wife and children revolve.

The glue of this arrangement works for some, although real intimacy is difficult to achieve among unequals on the level of either companionship or sexuality. For many the glue begins to wear thin. She experiences the emptiness of a satellite, of an unidentified object with no personal identity. He is either threatened by the menacing burden of her emptiness or else by the growing fear that his dependence on her dependence could be called into question. At this point the unwritten contract is in trouble.

The new marriage has its beginning in this questioning of the old mystiques. A sense of being threatened, probably felt by both persons, will be the initial impact of the questioning. To the extent that our feeling of adequacy as men is dependent on female dependence, we will feel disturbed and defensive when women call into question the mystique for which they have been programmed by society. Even the most constructive and liberating growth appears at first in the form of a death.

The new marriage comes to no person without resistance and struggle. But because the new marriage is the birth of an equal relationship through the death of the old mystiques, real intimacy is now actually possible. The new male and the new female can share a deeper commitment to Jesus Christ, a closer companionship, a healthier sexuality. There are more resources to share since both male and female are set free to participate in whatever functions are helpful to their mutual needs. Neither is cut off from part of the self by stereotyped straight jackets as to what male and female feelings and roles are supposed to be.

Through the new marriage, more complete models of adulthood are held before our children. Men become real parents, and women become real citizens of the world. With the increase of human potential that is an indispensable purpose of marriage, the community of the family is freed for missional care and concern toward others.

My wife and I began to experience a new marriage when we slowly but surely recognized that for us *a mystique plus a mystique equaled a mistake*. Not a mistake in the sense that we married each other, but in the same sense that a lifestyle of two mystiques is really more of a "death" style. The combination of two mystiques is a devastating formula for alienation, hostility, exploitation, manipulation, and competition. And make no mistake about it. The marriage of two mystiques is the classic pattern of our society. We perpetuate this union of mystiques in our patterns of rearing children and through our own images and expectations of ourselves and of others.

I believe the gospel of Jesus Christ is asking questions of us men. "Do I have to have a marriage where my wife is an accessory-like satellite, or do I welcome her identity as being through herself as my identity is through myself? Am I willing to be a nurturing parent of our children, or do I see this role as women's work? Can I move toward the reality of wider choices, not only for women in general, but for *my wife* in particular?" I find myself as concerned with my wife's development as a person as my own, and this means nitty-gritty tasks like car-pooling and taking my share of domestic responsibilities. By my doing so she is able to pursue goals that are important to her.

As we see the whirlpools of cultural change all around us, we glimpse a confluence of liberation coming our way. For the truth of the matter is that the liberation of another person is *my* liberation, too. Likewise the oppression of another person is oppression for me, too.

The new marriage is no idealistic, pre-established mold with a set of easy-to-follow instructions. Rather, it is a process by which persons struggle to break through debilitating mystiques into a new relationship of equality and enablement, a pattern that reflects the Lordship of Jesus Christ, the egalitarian exemplar of humankind. For in Jesus Christ there are neither male nor female mystiques, but male and female human beings.[13]

Through the new consciousness of the women's movement, I have discovered hidden facets of my own being. For example, I have learned how to *receive* from others, a posture frequently difficult for white males and especially for clergy. Not long ago a female member of our faculty gave me a flower for enjoyment in my office. It was the first time anyone had ever given me a flower. Impossible by the old stereotypes but delightful by the new humanness!

I have learned to get in touch with feelings at a new level and some of this I owe to the freedom of women to cry and to share deep longings. What this could mean if practiced openly and supportively by more white males! I have experienced the costly grace of greater involvement in the daily care that undergirds the entire fabric of our society—the care of dishes, transportation, dental appointments, and the like. Authority and power in society become arrogant and demonic when separated from the nurturing care that oils and greases the channels of daily life.

An amazing fact is that Abraham and Zacchaeus gave up their "have-it-made" status for the uncertain future to which God beckoned them. In that uncertainty was disclosed and discovered the only certainty of human existence. Sometimes we call this certainty the irrepressible grace of God. And sometimes we call this reality the unconditional love of God. Whatever words we use, we are pointing to the source and to the chief end or purpose of all life.

CHAPTER FIVE

Nurturing Life Systems
with People Priorities

"The future isn't what it used to be." These words scrawled in a subway station express the despairing nostalgia of much of humanity in the second half of the twentieth century. A rapidly multiplying population explosion, the prospects of nuclear blackmail, and the ominous approach of environmental exhaustion combine to offer an outlook of "a contingent life sentence."[1] These precarious conditions and others like them suggest a preview of coming afflictions according to a burgeoning array of futurologists, forecasters, and seers. All other considerations aside, the depletion of energy resources alone—resources that cannot be recycled or replenished—portends a shrinking set of expectations for a technological society. A drastic revision of the future is coming for all who are beneficiaries of the consumer society.

What we must not overlook, however, is that for another huge portion of humanity there is hopeful expectation in the words "the future isn't what it used to be." If the past has been characterized by suffering and marginal existence, it is good news if the future does not have to be a repeat of the past. What for one person is a statement of despair will for another be an expression of anticipation. Whether there is peril or promise depends on what our past has been, on what changes may come to pass, and on who we are becoming in the process of change.

In Chapter Four lifestyles were the center of our attention as we reconsidered some dimensions of the Good Life Redefined from a Christian perspective. Lifestyles cannot be separated from life systems any more than the air we breathe can be disassociated from the immediate ecological environment. The significance of this relationship is crucial, but it is one which we do not easily grasp due to the cultural glorification of individualism at the expense of community. Archbishop Helder Camara, mentioned in the previous chapter, has remarked that we can give aid to an individual and be called saints. But if we appeal for a systems change through justice, we may be called subversive.

The contradiction between personal humaneness and complicity in an evil system is pointed out in the example of Henry Bergh, one of the great humanitarians in nineteenth-century America. In 1865 Bergh organized the nation's first humane society, a New York group called the American Society for the Prevention of Cruelty to Animals. Yet he saw no conflict in prosecuting a person for cruelty to a horse or a dog while he and his wife dressed from head to toe in furs from the skins of many animals.[2]

In the hope that our lifestyles and life systems might become more consistent with one another, this chapter will focus on life systems, or as the New Testament might have named it, on powers and principalities.

As will be suggested in Chapter Six, God is as concerned with life systems as with lifestyles; with power and principalities as with prayer and personal piety; with the public realm as with the personal realm. Theologically, the basis of these claims is that God is the God of all creation, the God of social justice, the God incarnate in Jesus Christ who is Lord of all. To say less than this can mean only that either we have not been reading our Bibles or that we wish to proclaim the death of God in the public arenas of significant decision-making.

In this chapter I will lift up just one direction which privileged and prosperous Christians need to consider if we are to nurture a society and a world in which people matter more than any *thing*. As we embark on this brief journey, be advised that (1) I am writing to myself as well as to others, as has been the case throughout the book, (2) I believe these directions to be based on a biblical understanding of God's revelation in the prophets of social justice and in Jesus Christ.

The Economic Life System

"Economics plays a central role in shaping the activities of the modern world. . . . There is no other set of criteria that exercises greater influence over the actions of individuals and groups as well as over those of governments. . . . Economic performance, economic growth, economic expansion, and so forth have become the abiding interest, if not the obsession, of all modern societies."[3]

With these words the late E. F. Schumacher reminds us that economics has become the *organizing principle* around which much of today's life is focused. Insofar as the economic calculus becomes the overriding factor in determining human affairs, the condition of the market, so to speak, becomes a religion in and of itself. Instead of "Economics as if People Mattered" (E. F. Schumacher's subtitle to *Small is Beautiful*), the rule becomes People as if Economics Mattered. In biblical terms we might say that when economics becomes the organizing principle of life, it is equivalent to humanity existing for the sabbath rather than the sabbath for humanity.

The very importance of economics means that it is especially incumbent on privileged and prosperous Christians to develop a faith "system" that determines our economic practices rather than economic practices that determine our faith. It took me many years to grow a faith, through the grace of God, that determined my political posture—to replace a political perspective that dominated my Christian faith. Similarly, we need to be testing our economic assumptions and practices with a biblically grounded faith. Otherwise we will not be able to see beyond our own vested interests.

The relationship of Christian faith to the economic system has long been of special interest to me. I suppose it goes back to my initial educational and vocational experience as an adult. My first degree in higher education was a double major in banking, finance, and accounting. Following the first degree with a Masters in Business Management, I was then involved in the banking profession and the oil industry. For me the ordained ministry was a second vocational commitment.

What I discovered as a business professional was no more or less than any thinking business person knows in our society, especially if you have been exposed to the Christian faith as I had. Every one of us knows that there is some kind of contradiction between the demands of a highly competitive economic system and a faith that proclaims the priority of cooperation, community, and solidarity with others. In a system where the bottom line—rather than the effect on either people or nature—is *the* issue, it takes a well-honed repression to disguise the inevitable conflict with an ethic of love and compassion.

In fact I have often remarked that if taken seriously, the Christian faith will intensify our quandary at the intersection of competitive economics with a people ethic based on love. We usually handle this dilemma by presupposing that the system is "a given" of our existence or at least "better" than any alternative. Today, however, privileged and prosperous Christians need to look more openly and study more deeply the economic system in which we participate.

It is not easy for anyone to render judgment against a system from which one has personally benefited for a lifetime. The economic system of the United States has provided ample goods and material necessities. We have become accustomed to calling this "the world's highest standard of living." In addition, in my case, our economic system has provided a level of income more than sufficient for my needs. This has been true in the banking profession, the oil industry, and now in the ministry of the church as a theological administrator. There is no use denying that our ecclesiastical institutions are in large measure dependent on gifts from income derived through our present system.

In spite of these favorable experiences of a personal nature, which could be multiplied in the testimony of so many other persons as well, it has become painfully clear to me that privileged and prosperous Christians can no longer be the unprotesting beneficiaries of the present system. To think and act as Christians is to get on the Abrahamic road, to join the Zacchaean adventure. And this means that we move beyond self-interest as Christians to larger considerations and concerns. While I am sometimes suspicious of Christian interpretations that are overflowing with "oughts" and "musts," I have come to believe that Christians *must* reconsider our unquestioning affirmation of the present economic system because of the following factors.

A Predatory System

1. Our economic system is one that has resulted in an enormous disparity between haves and have-nots in spite of the greatest abundance of any civilization in history. With approximately 20 percent of our U.S. citizens mired in a marginal situation of economic survival, thousands enjoy multiple homes and bank accounts and virtually an unlimited consumer capacity. That this situation is even possible is a disgrace for a nation of over 60 million citizens who call ourselves Christians. Our economic system is predatory in the sense that the small and the weak are devoured by corporate giants whose use of power is dictated by the demands of the bottom line.

Cybernated glory replaces human labor because it is more efficient and because our economic system calls for a definition of efficiency in terms of dollars rather than human need. If a corporate board of directors must choose between the public good and making a profit for the stockholders, is it not expected that the latter will nearly always prevail because that is the very nature of our system?

2. I have not referred to our system as free enterprise because as anyone familiar with our economy knows we do not have free enterprise. What we do have is a maze of regulations that tend to favor those who

have lobbying strength over those who have no counsel in the councils of legislative power. When the powerless receive government aid, we call it welfare. When those engaged in transportation and other industries receive government aid, we call it subsidies. Some will argue that it is appropriate to give subsidies to those who can make a contribution to our society since it is in the public interest to do so. However, if we were to take seriously the biblical perspective that *everything* belongs to God, we could not neatly divide up the population into the deserving and the nondeserving, the productive and the nonproductive. Furthermore, what we have heretofore called contributive or "productive" may in fact be counterproductive to the urgent interests of humanity.

3. We pride ourselves on the efficiency of competition, a method that supposedly results in the best of goods and services. But how can we claim to be efficient in a global sense when something like 40 percent of the earth's resources are consumed for 6 percent of the world's population? How can we point to efficiency when fewer and fewer goods are made to last but are assumed to be disposable at will? What definition of competence is being used when the atmosphere and the waterways are polluted and endangered at unprecedented rates? And what can we mean by a high standard of living when it is partially based on the standard of cheap labor and exploitation of resources from Third World countries? All of these smack of predatory means and ends and should be questioned by those who understand themselves in the biblical tradition.

4. Our present system is predatory because it is based on the plunder of nature. No one to my knowledge has shown more convincingly than E. F. Schumacher that a fundamental cornerstone of American economic theory in recent decades is now turning to dust. I refer to the arrogant assumption that the earth's resources are unlimited and that therefore the problem of production has been solved.

"A businessman would not consider a firm to have solved its problems of production and to have achieved viability if he saw that it was rapidly consuming its capital. How, then, could we overlook this vital fact when it comes to that very big firm, the economy of spaceship Earth and, in particular, the economics of its rich passengers?"[4] Schumacher is telling us that economists of all stripes have become victims of an illusion, namely the failure to distinguish between income and capital. The capital provided by nature is much more significant and fundamental than the capital provided by humans. "This larger part (capital provided by nature) is now being used up at an alarming rate and that is why it is an absurd and suicidal error to believe, and act on the belief, that the problem of production has been solved."[5]

I am convinced that Schumacher's insight is so undeniable that we *must* rethink the whole basis of our economic system *even if up to now and apart from the ecological question we still believe that the assets outweigh the liabilities—even including the dehumanizing effects of the system on other human beings.* If it becomes clear, as I believe is now being revealed to us in our moment of history, that our economic system is becoming a failure in its "success," *we must* radically revamp the very foundations. If our "highest standard of living in the world" is in fact a bittersweet achievement rapidly exploiting unrepeatable natural resources, our choice is destruction of life and nature or a rethinking and redoing of our economic heritage.

Unless economic theory functions within a larger vision of what Schumacher calls "metaphysics or meta-economics," it is destined for a utilitarian role that plays havoc with the environment and that reduces the earth's resources to a private playground for predatory appropriation. Theodore Roszak says it well in his introduction to *Small Is Beautiful:* "We need a nobler economics that is not afraid to discuss spirit and conscience, moral purpose and the meaning of life, an economics that aims to educate and elevate people, not merely to measure their low-grade behavior."[6]

Getting on the Church's Agenda

If the church is to explore the contradictions of our present economic system with the presuppositions of Christian faith, the first step is inclusion on the agenda. At the present time the very questioning of the economic question is hardly seen as permissible on the level of the local church. There is a "sacred cow" aura surrounding the capitalistic system as though it were off limits as a faith question.

If I were to recall the two areas where I have most often experienced a division of the house between clergy and laity, I would name the issue of economics and faith and that of politics and faith. My father used to say that he expected preachers to be a bit more "on the socialistic side," as he put it. His rationale was that ministers spent most of their time with the needs of people whereas the laity were more likely to be caught up with the concern of profit-making. Besides, he mused, if preachers were all that interested in making money they would have responded to a profit orientation rather than to a service motif.

His point was not that lay persons are greedy profiteers unconcerned for people. He was merely pointing to the fact that many church members spend a great deal of time and effort in roles directly related to profit and loss matters. Since this is in fact the case, the vast majority of pastors are not well educated in economic theory and thus do not feel comfortable in leading efforts to explore our economic system from the standpoint of their faith.

I believe that what needs to happen is for pastors to help lay persons examine the biblical perspective on ownership, land, and natural environment. We need to make available the biblical resources in rethinking our assumptions about the economic system. I do not have a system of sophisticated balance-of-power theories to recommend for immediate use. What I do believe is that no change is even possible unless there is a pervasive attitudinal change in the religious, professional, and educational sectors of our society. Only as a radical shaking of the foundations rises to the forefront of public consciousness will an alternative system become possible. "Success cannot be obtained by some form of magic produced by scientists, technicians, or economic planners. It can come only through a process of growth involving the education, organization, and discipline of the whole population. Anything less than this must end in failure."[7]

If the church is to be a part of a widespread shift in economic attitudes, we need not wait until we have a finalized plan of action. Indeed, our task is not to become the social engineers but the questioners of the existing moral ethos and the advocates of a new order with more humane priorities. Our task is to see that the key issues are given a hearing on our own agenda, and insofar as possible, on public agendas. Our hearing cannot take place without candid discussions about the role of economics in the world today, nor without an examination of biblical perspectives. It is this latter concern to which I now call your attention.

The Biblical Calculus: God's Public Enterprise

The church is called of God to hold two realities in creative interaction. One is the Word of God, our wellspring and touchstone. The other is the word of the world, that is, the way things presently are. We look at the Word. We look at the world. Then we imagine what can be through the grace of God, knowing that even our best vision is partial and incomplete. When we look at economics through the eyes of the Bible, what attitudes and alternatives come into view? What kind of fabric of social care might be woven into our economic life? What might it look like to nurture an economic system with greater emphasis on human beings and with a changing relationship to nature? Let me try you on some ruminations.

The basic and unfailing position of the Bible is that God is the creator and owner of everything. The earth is the Lord's and those who dwell therein, an emphasis particularly strong in the Genesis creation stories and in the Psalms. Since God is the owner of everything, we are not the true owners. We are stewards for property, land, or other assets that belong to God and that are to be used for the good of all. The point of the Parable of the Rich Fool in Luke 12:13-21 is that God is the true owner of crops and the barns which hold them.

The biblical perspective, then, is that our possessions are not truly or ultimately ours. When we use personal pronouns, we do so in the Christian faith only in a pilgrimatic way to suggest our temporary steward-ship. Indeed, the rites of baptism often conspicuously and deliberately remind us that "our" children are actually God's, not ours. Likewise in the service of matrimony. We do not own another person. Each belongs to God in the most profound sense. To obscure these truths is to dese-crate the personhood of another human person and at the same time elevate ourselves into a false and idolatrous position.

The critical issue at stake here is that as far as the Bible is concerned, there is no private ownership that is not responsible to the common good as a trust or stewardship for God. To reduce economics to so-called private enterprise is a theological contradiction of the first order. In the Bible all economic relationships are of the nature of God's public enter-prise, that is, a life system that is supportive of the entire community as a representation of God's gifts in creation.

There is no place in either the Old or the New Testament in which the private appropriation for one's own benefit apart from the common good receives the blessings of God.

God's ownership of everything, including what we call capital, labor, and the means of production, means that our relationship to the earth is to be one of enduring reverence rather than exploitation and blatant depletion. From the Genesis 2 creation account we recall that the first human is "to till it and keep it" (v. 15). In a paper entitled "World Hunger from the Biblical Perspective," Charles Baughman has enabled me to see more clearly the Hebrew roots in the above passage. "The word trans-lated 'till' is *avadah,* which means 'to serve' and is used also to mean 'to worship.' The Hebrew word translated 'keep' is *shamar* and means 'to watch over' and 'to guard.' Both of these words, it seems to me, set the tone for the rest of the biblical understanding of how human beings are to be related to the earth/land and its inhabitants."[8]

If we grant that the above critique of a biblical posture is essentially correct, what can it mean for our society? Other than its implications for some individual lifestyles of privileged and prosperous Christians, does it have any social import or impact for the economic and political powers that be? I believe that it does.

We are approaching a time in history when the Truth is moving in on us as never before. In our own day God is destroying the wisdom of the wise and thwarting the cleverness of the clever (1 Cor. 1:19). Whole systems that have been assumed to be the marks of an advanced civilization and of a high standard of living are now exposed as a Jekyll and Hyde combination. Our economic development is just one example in a society that is already passing from modernity to a post-technological era.

While the spectre of new limits may serve only to bring about a new wave of selfishness and security consciousness in peoples and systems, it is also the case that a new pragmatism may be engendered. Our global village is at least aware as never before of the global interconnectedness linking all human beings in a common destiny with the earth and its environment. The poor and the powerless may "go first," but an earth stripped of its life-giving qualities will destroy *all* human defenses. So it becomes a matter of pragmatic self-interest to make some changes.

My own hope is that a merger of religious consciousness and pragmatic realism will begin to bring about seismic shocks in the human consciousness. Whether we have the resources of will and imagination to translate such a new human consciousness into economic and political realities remains to be seen. As indicated in the preface, this book centers more on attitudes as may be influenced by the biblical view of life than on the complex social balance of power by which these attitudes may be translated into social reality.

As already suggested, I do not believe that in our system of government much radically new social engineering will take place unless undergirded by significant shifts in basic assumptions and priorities on a rather widespread basis. The theme of this book, that is, the liberation of privileged and prosperous Christians, indicates some of the directions that I believe are necessary to qualify for significant attitudinal change.

The biblical calculus for the realm of economics is one that emphasizes the sovereignty of God over the entire creation. A standard of living by a biblical perspective will not be measured by the Gross National Product, the consumer index, or the Dow-Jones Industrial Averages. It will have to do with how faithful we earth people are in providing the bounties of the earth for all the earth's citizens, and how faithful we are in restraint and replenishment of the earth's bounties.

If the biblical perspective on economics were to become influential in our economic system, it might lead to people priorities like these:

1. The business and economic community would incur a dramatic increase in social responsibility and a corresponding decrease in excessive profits and personal wealth. Private interests would be subordinated to public requirements. This trend could be made possible by limitations

on multinational corporations in terms of size, profits, and geographical territory. Severe penalties would be invoked for crimes against nature, such as air and water pollution. Major tax reforms would put a ceiling on profits and call for taxation *before* profits as well as after in order to recognize the indebtedness of the private sector to public expenditure from which the former draws benefits. For example the public purse finances a significant percentage of higher education from which industry draws its leadership. Public expenditure makes possible federal systems of transportation, including highways and subsidies to the air carriers upon which corporate executives are quite dependent. Many other examples could be offered.

We cannot afford an economic operation that is long on profits and short on social care. As Gandhi said, "Earth provides enough to satisfy *every* person's need, but not for *every* person's greed."[9] Private ownership divorced from work enables owners to live parasitically on the labor of others. Thus, our laws and regulations should encourage the merger of ownership and work and discourage large-scale enterprises that separate the two.

We have too long defined freedom as the license to pursue personal advantage instead of the responsibility to contribute to the common good. The rise of large-scale corporate capitalism encourages authoritarian rather than democratic tendencies. As such it is inimical to both a biblical view of life and the intention of individual participation in one's destiny envisioned by our American predecessors. Big business and big government support one another in an incestuous relationship that encourages narrow self-interest and thus works against the public good. A system of profit maximization is a fool's paradise even for those who reap the financial rewards.

2. A larger percentage of public monies would be spent on human needs, with a corresponding decrease in military and defense spending. This is easier said than done as is discovered by those presidential candidates who subsequently find themselves in the White House. While our cities decay and the needs of citizens go wanting, we continue to pour billions of dollars into weaponry, much of which is outdated by the time it comes off the assembly line. Our insatiable appetite for military hardware is a menace to quality of life and to the true internal security of our country.

In February 1976 a representative of the Friends Committee on National Legislation testified before the House Budget Committee on the Fiscal 1977 Budget. Excerpts from this testimony express the concerns that I believe should typify the biblical community of faith:

Most witnesses before this Committee will probably stress economic, political, military, and security factors. These are important, but we think there is another dimension which should also be considered for a rounded picture. We must look at the budget in the light of moral and ethical considerations and in the context of human needs at home and around the world as well.

I am not coming before you with a detailed definition of moral and ethical requirements in today's complex world. But I do believe it is fair to say that there is a general obligation falling upon us citizens acting together through our government to try to assure that all people in our country have reasonable access at least to the minimum basics for a decent life—food, shelter, education, health care, a job. I believe it is generally accepted also that we in the United States, who have been generously endowed with material resources, a favorable climate, and an energetic people, have a responsibility toward those in less fortunate circumstances around the world.

We are also counseled to choose life-supporting rather than death-dealing policies, to turn away from war and toward peace, to practice justice, and to care for the sick and the elderly.

When we set these requirements against the world's needs and our domestic needs—hunger, malnutrition, disease, poverty, inequity, threats to our environment, population growth, resource depletion, to name a few—we confront a tremendous challenge.

The federal budget is perhaps the best available evidence of what our national values really are, of how we as a people attempt to cope with our challenges and responsibilities in the world.

Using this yardstick, we believe that this budget, if accepted as proposed, would constitute a severe indictment of our nation. It is preoccupied with weaponry and war. It proposes spending $114.9 billion on "national defense." It shortchanges the poor, the elderly, the sick, and others in need. It increases military spending though tensions are easing. It decreases domestic programs, though millions are without jobs, nutritious food, good health care, adequate housing, and other necessities of life.

MILITARY PROGRAMS UP; NON-MILITARY PROGRAMS DOWN

To indicate some of the reasons we draw this conclusion, we have juxtaposed below various weapons programs which are being increased in FY1977 with various non-military programs.

Headstart programs reduced $20 million to (a decreased total
  of) $434 million
Six AWACS surveillance and command aircraft increased $120
  million to $584 million
Maternal and child health services reduced $112 million to $210
  million
One AS submarine tender to support nuclear attack submarines
  increased from $0.5 million to $263 million
Soil Conservation Service reduced $26 million to $402 million
Sixteen F-16 air combat fighters, increased $404 million to $620
  million
Legal Services for the poor reduced $8 million to $80 million
Strike cruiser— nuclear powered, increased $188 million to
  $203 million
General mental health centers reduced $88 million to $131
  million
Army XM-1 Tank System increased $89 million to $141 million
Multilateral development assistance reduced $300 million to
  $1,205 million
Eight guided missile frigates increased $318 million to $1,282
  million
Cancer research, reduced $55 million to $688 million
One hundred A-10 attack aircraft, increased $141 million to
  $617 million.[10]

The kinds of alternatives that I have been lifting up are on the order of
clues, provocative possibilities, and impressionistic images. Any sea-
soned reader, especially in the discipline of economics, will recognize the
fact that every suggestion for an alternative step brings with it a new set of
questions, rebuttals, and dilemmas. I am not so much proposing fixed
answers as I am raising the kinds of questions that must be worked
through if we are to have a future worth imagining and living.

In summation of this section, I am saying that our task is to discover an
economic design, whatever the label, that redefines freedom as the
responsibility to contribute to the common good instead of as a privilege
for personal acquisition. A design supportive of people priorities will aim
at the maximization of responsible environmental stewardship instead of
maximization of profits; it will appreciate smallness and individuality while
depreciating vast corporate systems which depersonalize; it will regard
food and other necessities as a human right, just as we now regard public
education as a fundamental right; it will learn to appreciate growth in

terms of human values rather than in terms of production or profits; it will think within a global perspective rather than a national one; it will increasingly understand the relationship between national security and people priorities; and it will explore the meaning of work and its relationship to other values, such as cultural, social, and esthetic.

Even for privileged and prosperous Christians who have reaped the spoils of our present economic system in a world in which poor Lazarus is legion, perhaps a more sober future is preferable to no future at all. Whether our motivation is Christian solidarity with the legion of Lazarus for the sake of our common liberation, or a pragmatic realization that the present economic ship is a titanic one, the future isn't what it used to be.[11] And for that we should give thanks in our moments of faith to the One who creates all, owns all, and in whom the economic system is intended to be a public enterprise for the well-being of all.

People Priorities as a Clue to Other Life Systems

My hope for this chapter is that it will be provocative not only in relation to the economic life system, but also in connection with other systems. In other words the reader might translate the approach of this chapter to the political life system, the other system that I regard as terribly consequential for privileged and prosperous Christians. My method has been to analyze briefly what seems to me to be the basic gestalt of our present system (predatory), to review several fundamental biblical assumptions about economics, and to follow up with some inquiries and pointers for future directions.

Something like this, I believe, is our assignment as the Christian community in addressing the Christian message to all the present systems in which we participate. I regard this assignment as especially imperative for the economic and political systems of our time because of the enormous power over life combined in the two. If Christians do not want the God of the Bible squarely in the midst of these powers and principalities, our prayers can only be insidious attempts to use "in Jesus' name" for personal aggrandizement.

In the inside cover jacket of Margaret Mitchell's epic novel, Gone with the Wind, we are told that this is a story that centers around Scarlett O'Hara, "who arrives at young womanhood just in time to see the Civil War sweep away the life for which her upbringing had prepared her." We, too, are beginning to experience the demise of those life systems for which our past has prepared us. It's time to nurture new life systems with people priorities.

CHAPTER SIX

Improvisations on Liberation and Evangelism

To be faithful to our biblical heritage and to be adequate for our time, theological reflection must come to terms with an understanding of evangelism. Theologies of liberation are no exception, regardless of whether they speak for the powerless or the privileged and the prosperous. The indispensability of evangelism as the core of any theology should become apparent as this chapter progresses.

Anyone who has been around the Christian community for even a brief spell knows that the *evangelion,* the good news or glad tidings of Jesus Christ, is understood in radically different ways. To get straight to the point, one position maintains what some refer to as an "evangelism stance." This view holds that the one essential purpose of God through the gospel has to do with "saving souls." A conflicting position is taken by the "liberation stance." It claims that the good news is God's redemptive action not only in individual lives but in the political and economic arenas of history in which human beings live their lives. When we listen, this is what we hear: "They do not believe that God is Lord of all life, but only of the private, individual life of the believer." Or this: "They make the gospel into a social and political matter rather than the transformation of the self through God's grace in any and all circumstances."

In this chapter I propose first of all to suggest a sketch of evangelism that might do justice to New Testament means and modalities. Second, I will offer some New Testament *guidelines* for evangelism in relation to liberation theologies that I believe are essential for the faithful and effective functioning of Christian evangelism itself. These guidelines will have a special importance for a liberation theology for privileged and prosperous Christians.

New Testament Images of Evangelism

In our time evangelism too often has come to mean a sales technique in a mass rally. Or the church serving its own needs. Or an arrogant attempt to point out the most superior religion of all. For Jesus and for the initial Christian community that proclaimed him as Lord, evangelism was something else.

For Jesus the Good News was the kingdom of God breaking into human affairs. The kingdom came as a gift; it called for radical dependence on the grace of God as the foundation and framework for one's existence and self-understanding, and further called for recognition of the kingdom's claim upon us to love our neighbors. As we shall see, Jesus made use of many means to point to the kingdom of God as the decisive factor in human existence.

For the New Testament church Jesus himself became the enfleshment of the kingdom of God. Thus the presence and action of God in Jesus as Lord of all life became the focus of evangelism. Evangelism was not a departmentalized activity among other activities. Evangelism was the church confessing its faith and doing so in a variety of ways. The church's confession was an affirmation that in God's love through Jesus Christ the world has experienced the root reality of the cosmos: the everlasting, unconditional love by which we are brought into being and in which we live and move and have our being forever. This root of all roots is given to all human beings as the ground and object of their lives, both interior and exterior, individually and in community.

The church's confession is consummated in the further affirmation, inseparable from the first, that because of God's love and in the power of that love we are to love all others in the light of God's love for them, as most strikingly revealed through Jesus Christ. As Paul Tillich reminded us so well, the confession of Jesus as the Christ is not a claim to superiority. It is an acknowledgment of a gift; a recognition of the hallowedness of all life; a reconciliation with God and thus with self and neighbor; a pointing to the new being for whom faith working through love is the essence of life. I believe that in the New Testament this is what evangelism is about.

With this in mind let us now reflect on some images of evangelism in the New Testament.

Extolment Evangelism. Electronic communication has made us wary of "messages" and advocacy in the form of advertisements. People may listen when E. F. Hutton speaks, at least a few times. But for the most part only a zealot-like intentionality to see a program through can withstand the onslaught of inane commercial persuasions. The exchange rate on the spoken word is rendered cheap, so that not a few are convinced that persuasion can genuinely come only through the efficacy of relationships or the power of the deed.

In spite of the fractured and devalued spoken word, communication theorists and language specialists continue to insist that the shape of reality is a verbal one.[1] Central to human communication is the spoken word. It is this capacity for verbal symbols and of obtaining a response as a result that is one mark of the uniqueness of human beings. These insights were presupposed in the Protestant Reformation that recovered the spoken word and the corresponding truth that faith is always a matter of *hearing* the Gospel (Luther).

For me an unforgettable dramatization of the necessity of oral trans-mission was offered in the film *Fahrenheit 451*. Depicting a 1984-type setting in which books are forbidden and destroyed by the state, the unfolding story centers around a remnant community whose common memory is the last depository of countless books. With all libraries and personal collections eliminated, only the prodigious memory of this small group protects the world's written masterpieces from permanent obliv-ion.

In a particularly memorable scene an aged and dying man is urgently going over the last few lines of *David Copperfield* with a young boy, all from memory. It is obvious that the old man is the only living receptacle of this particular book and that the book's future for all time now precari-ously depends on the successful completion of the oral transmission into the memory of the youth. A race against time!

Even with the availability of countless books, including the Bible, we know that the Christian tradition is passed from one generation to another by word of mouth. The spoken word is the fulcrum of Christian confession. Just as we cannot learn to speak as human beings unless we have first been spoken to by others, we cannot comprehend or embrace the Christian gospel unless someone has already spoken it to us.

Extolment evangelism is the church confessing its faith, that is, pointing to the evangel through human speech. This evangelism of the Word through words is naming the name and telling the story in order to elicit a response. To extol is to lift up, to laud or praise highly. Extolment may take place in the form of pulpit proclamation or in the advocacy of a Christian to another human being. Whatever the form, setting, and style, the evangel is extolled in the verbal symbols of human speech.

The message of Jesus was an extolment of the coming kingdom of God, already breaking in upon human existence. He used parables and all manner of story to lift up the action of God in history. He was not a silent man, although he knew solitude. He was an itinerant preacher, proclaimer, extoller of God's Word through words.

We need little or no reminder that the initial history of the church is a history of spoken advocacy. "We cannot but speak of what we have seen and heard" (Acts 4:20). "Go and stand in the temple and speak to the people all the words of this Life" (Acts 5:20). "And everyday in the temple and at home they did not cease teaching and preaching Jesus as the Christ" (Acts 5:42). These passages from Acts will speak for the New Testament church.

We have been reminded by the black church experience that the signal test of the minister is, "Can he or she tell the story?," that is, the story of Jesus Christ as it relates to the history, experience, and needs of the black brothers and sisters. As one black lay person told me, "When necessary we can forgive our ministers for just about anything except failure to tell the story with urgency and power." This is not intended to presuppose a black preacher for a black congregation, but it does hold before us a historic expectation.

The extolling function is necessary for the faith community's reappropriation of its identity and reason for being. The Word of God, when true and lively in its proclamation, holds before us the ultimate, universal, and unifying promise and claim of God's love in Jesus Christ. Evangelism takes place in the announcing of the life-giving Word.

The church has too often defined evangelism strictly in te ns of the unchurched. But Jesus spoke the word of God again and again not only to the multitude but also to the disciples as well. The preacher's task is one of evangelism, speaking the Word of God to the People of God who gather as the representatives of all humanity—God's people. I intend no depreciation of the Christian community when I say what most of us already know but too seldom admit: when I compare some of the folks inside our walls with some who are outside, a comparison which begins with myself, I have no doubt about the fact that Sunday morning proclamation is indeed an evangelistic function!

Whether the setting is corporate or one-to-one, the extolment of the Gospel is in essence an exultation that bears glad tidings in a world of misery, alienation, and despair. Through words the Word is lifted up. Through words the Word calls for a decision in response.

Edification Evangelism. Our Lord was more than an itinerant preacher as far as evangelistic methods were concerned. The immediate disciples, having responded to his proclamation that the kingdom of God is at hand, were exposed to intensive training in discipleship. We can hardly imagine the teaching, the searching, the questing that was an ongoing part of their association with Jesus for something like a three-year period. By the lakeside. In lonely places. Amid the multitudes. On the road. It was not by accident that Jesus was called "Rabboni," that is, teacher!

Edification evangelism is the task of understanding, linking, and sorting out the implications of gospel extolment and acceptance. John Wesley was a genius in conserving the results of preaching through the Methodist classes. What he did in this connection was patterned after Jesus' example with the disciples. As I reflect on the widespread loss of membership within several Protestant communions during the 1970s, I wonder how many new members were involved in having their roots deepened and nourished through an adult education process. Or were they members in name only? Does not the term "disciple" mean one who searches and learns?

It has been said that theological students used to come to seminary with faith, but that now they come with hope. Making room for the over-simplification, there is accuracy in the insight. Our edification level in the church is so low and fragmented that we cannot assume a coherent beginning knowledge of Christian doctrine, history, or biblical narra-tive—even in those who are to become, we hope, the ordained ministers of the church.

Given the current situation throughout the church in adult education, who can claim that the teaching function, with all of its difficulties, is less than a form and function of Christian evangelism? Edification evan-gelism is an indispensable means of equipping the people of God for both an informed and a transformed ministry in the world. If it is true that less than 3 percent of the people who record decisions are found in churches as active disciples six months later, our evangelism surely best be concerned with retention and conservation.[2] The evangelism of the extolled Word needs the evangelism of the edifying Word.

Empathic Evangelism. Henri J. M. Nouwen has said that the first vocation of the Christian is to care. There is no more powerful form of evangelism than the outreaching love of a Christian to another human being. All of us, whether clergy or lay, have seen persons radically changed through the empathic identification of one person with another. Within every congregation there are enormous gifts of caring that find their expression through small groups and within a one-to-one context. Reuel Howe has reminded us that "the Gospel is a saving event that occurs in human relations and is not a body of knowledge for mere verbal transmission."[3] The medium of empathic evangelism is that of relationship, of I-Thou, which of course involves the spoken word.

The empathic relationship characterized the ministry of Jesus as he identified with the hurts and misery around him. His ministry of healing care and compassion is the basis of care in the church in every generation. How many times through the years have I seen the caring function of Christ exercised between lay persons in the church, or from a member or group of the congregation to a stranger in the community! A cup of water or a cup of chicken soup. The long wait in the night, sharing the anguish and the hope. The caring presence when there is little or nothing to say. Whatever the form, the place, the style—in relationships of care the Word becomes real in our lives anew.

These experiences, however, are not the ultimate ground of grace. They point to the transcendent giver of all gifts, the one whose grace is the fountain of all graces. I believe it was Viktor Frankl who said that only through finite relationships can we be freed *from* the finite *for* the finite, and thus be rooted in the infinite.

Empathic evangelism also occurs when the church listens to those who are disenchanted with the church. In a joint Lutheran-Catholic study, "Who Are the Unchurched?" (published by the Glenmary Research Center, Bethesda, Md.), the need for the church to listen to the unchurched was unmistakably clear. Many unchurched persons who were interviewed revealed a deep doubt that the church would listen seriously to their feelings and viewpoints. Empathic evangelism includes a ministry of the ear in which active and caring listening precedes evangelism of the mouth. I suspect that if the church is to move beyond intramural evangelism within our own ranks, as important as that is, we will do well to do more listening than we have been doing. Listening presupposes that we have something to learn and that the unchurched have gifts to give which we need to receive. And this presupposes that, thank God, we do not have a monopoly on the presence and action of the God who is loose in the world!

Exemplary Evangelism. Closely related to empathic evangelism is exemplary evangelism. The former, as I see it and interpret it, has to do with relationship, meeting, encounter, and also with the ear. The latter has to do with what we observe about another human being, or vice versa. Most of the people who are influenced by our lives are those who are involved with us in some personal way. But it is also the case that we have an impact, for better or worse, on some persons whom we never know in a personal way. They may observe us, or hear about us, or know of us, but never in a personal relationship. Exemplary evangelism is an evangelism of being and becoming.

We might say that there are those persons whose lives have an impact on ours as examples, models, illustrations, of what it means to be a human being. Not infrequently we read of a dying child or youth whose sports hero had no knowledge of the impact of his or her example. My point is that all around us and in us as well, life is being shaped. Life is looking at life. Someone will be regarded, for better or for worse, as an exemplary model for life. The result will be exemplification followed by emulation.

I have pictured Jesus as a preacher and as a teacher. We know, too, that people were drawn to him by his relationship of healing love and care for persons, and by his empathic solidarity with their life situation. As Jesus moved through city throngs and countryside crowds, there were many who no doubt never knew him in a personal sense. But they knew who he was and what he was about in his mission. The expanding concentric circles of his life reached out and touched the lives of many. They had observed faith working through love and resolved that their observations must become personal participation.

Sometimes our exemplary models are persons who lived in prior generations. The communion of saints comes alive as their faith speaks to our faith. Sometimes the exemplary life is from our own generation, both living and dead. Who can seriously doubt, for example, the exemplary role of the late Dr. Martin Luther King, Jr., for countless black youth and white persons as well who never knew him personally? As people look at your life and mine, what do they see? In the above mentioned study, "Who Are the Unchurched?," many unchurched persons indicated that they could see no difference between church members and other people. While this claim could be an easy excuse, it should give us pause for concern and reflection.

Before proceeding to another means of evangelism I want to comment on our Christian vocabulary. By now most readers will be exclaiming, "What is here called evangelism is no more than what the church has always been up to—preaching, teaching, community, service." Or kerygma, didache, koinonia, and diakonia. Exactly! If the church's one and only reason for being is to bear witness to the unconditional and everlasting love of God as the first, foremost, and last promise and claim of human existence, *everything* we do as church is a form of evangelism. There isn't anything we do that *isn't* evangelism, that is, pointing by word and deed to the evangelion, the good news of God in Christ. If we are involved in matters and tasks that are *not* evangelistic, they are at best irrelevant and at worst apostasy.

All of this means that the evangelion, the Good News, is our one and only "business." And this means that everything from the way we handle money as a church or institution of the church to the way we administer the community of faith is a theological task of evangelism. The Lordship of Jesus Christ is not compartmentalized, but universalized. The resurrection meant that instead of seeing Jesus nowhere since the Crucifixion, the disciples saw God everywhere! So the church has just this one reason for being: to point in word and deed to the evangel! Too often we have reduced evangelism into the narrow mold of bringing those "outside the church" into church membership. As Albert Outler comments on John Wesley, "He understood, as we had better, that a vital part of the church's evangelistic mission is—to herself."[4]

Ethical Evangelism. Ethical evangelism has a dual meaning. The first has to do with *the content* of the already mentioned forms of evangelism, especially extolment evangelism, as well as what I am presently going to call *enlistment* evangelism. In this first meaning the crux of the matter is the adequacy of the evangel content that is communicated. The second meaning of ethical evangelism is the manner in which the church demonstrates before the world the content of the Good News.

What I am calling ethical evangelism moves beyond the safe, popular, cultural images and interpretations of Jesus Christ. The church has whittled down the biblical witness to Jesus until any resemblance between the Jesus of the four gospels and the Jesus frequently proclaimed by the church is almost strictly coincidental! Where is the Jesus who blessed the peacemakers? The Jesus who championed the cause of the powerless and the poor? The Jesus whose kingdom reversed our worldly calculations and calibrations? The Jesus for whom community with God and neighbor was more important than acquisition and ownership? Dare we point to that evangelion?

In our proclamations and in our recruitment for new members, the demand of simple honesty requires us to make clear *who Jesus is* and what people are signing up for if they confess Jesus as Lord. While discipleship by its very nature entails growth, sanctification, and new discoveries of the all-encompassing Good News, it is just as true that an accurate portrayal of the gospel to begin with is necessary to avoid betrayal.

Obviously not every sermon and song can bear the entire scope of the gospel. Not every discussion can range from Advent to Epiphany to Pentecost. But any congregation that is not peddling cheap grace can communicate with clarity the gospel that calls into question our racism, sexism, and economic imperialism. Then people can make an informed choice about Jesus Christ and his body in the world.

If the whole evangel is not at least implied at the outset, why should we expect it to be included later? If the foolishness or stumbling block of the gospel is not proclaimed as a basis for commitment, how can it become a building block of commitment later? It is not enough merely to confess "Jesus Christ is Lord," calling that salvation. We confess a very particular Jesus Christ who revealed in very particular ways God's special concern for the oppressed. Only as *that* confession takes form in our lives should we think of ourselves as redeemed sinners in the company of Christ.

When I was pastor of Northaven United Methodist Church in Dallas, the evangelism-membership committee sponsored a monthly Sunday evening session for persons interested in exploring congregational membership. Participants had usually visited and worshipped several times and had received written material describing the congregation's various ministries. The material included a Northaven Profile, a booklet describing our ministry for the coming year. On the cover were these words: "The following pages provide, at best, a profile and some images of our intentions and directions for the year. The congregation is hereby reminded of its own intentionality, and other interested persons are provided insights into our self-understanding and priorities as a congregation."

One section of the booklet (an inexpensive mimeographed pamphlet) was entitled "The World's Agenda: The Struggle for Justice, Peace, and Freedom." A couple of paragraphs will suffice to provide an idea of its direction:

> If we ask "Who is God and what is God doing?," we might well answer that God is the giver of historical openings which bring possibilities of justice, peace, freedom, and human dignity. Biblically speaking, this is who God is, and this is what God is "up to." Our task as the Church, among other things, is to discern these openings and to move into them with redemptive concern and action. To do so is to appropriate the reality of becoming the Exodus-Easter community of faith. And so—as a congregation we look for those ways by which we can become participants in God's re-creative work in the struggle for human rights.
>
> Today many white suburbanites have begun to realize that we must begin with ourselves and our suburban neighbors as we seek solutions for the nation's overwhelming problems. We have begun to see the inner city as a mirror of who and what we have been, a disturbing reminder of our inverted priorities. Consequently, a great deal of the mission of the suburban church must first be directed at its own attitudes, its own values, its own neighborhood.

The style and shape of much of our congregational life in the form of worship, education, and corporate life thrusts in the direction of self-examination and renewal. Only as we attempt to be faithful in this task can we even begin to assume the role of servant of justice and reconciliation.

Following the introductory paragraphs, there followed brief descriptions of missional involvements in Project Equality, the Greater Dallas Housing Opportunities Center, Common Cause, a rehabilitation center for persons released from state prison, a medical center involving Native Americans, and other tasks to which we believed God was calling us.

The monthly session with inquirers afforded the congregation a chance to interpret through *both* pastor and laity the congregation's understanding and commitment to the gospel. In doing so our hope was to clarify the nature of the commitment being considered. While no specific program needed to be affirmed, it was made clear that we understood faith in God through Jesus Christ to mean an openness to the needs of the outcasts and the oppressed and a willingness to explore the implications. After all, why should a new church member be expected to respond with sensitivity to the concern of minorities if these concerns were in no way lifted up as having to do with discipleship in the first place? Why should we expect any kind of prophetic life from the church if our enlistment means and ends do no more than call people to salvation by conformity and creedal affirmations?

I've often maintained that if a visitor from outer space were to observe our preparation for Christmas without prior knowledge of the originating event, there would be no way that a true connection could be surmised. For how could such a visitor possibly conclude that the frenzied orgy of consumerism in December prepares for the birth of the babe in the manger, the Prince of Peace, the Lord of Love? How can prospective members fed on a diet of simplistic promises be expected to turn into a fellowship of risk-takers? How can a membership campaign that features positive thinking for the privileged and the prosperous regenerate into an outreaching love for the social and economic lepers of the world?

Evangelism is escapist if it has nothing to say to the affluence of the privileged and prosperous amid Third World starvation. Evangelism is expedient when it traffics in easy formulas and safe doctrines instead of calling us to a discipleship of transformed values. If evangelism conceals the cost of discipleship when it should reveal the call to obedience, are we going to rejoice in a quantitative kingdom of business as usual?

In the total witness of the church if we do not proclaim Jesus Christ, the *whole* Jesus Christ, and nothing but Jesus Christ, people are lured into our congregations under false pretenses. If Jesus' commitment to the powerless and downtrodden is not included in our total interpretive mosaic, then whatever we are saying and doing is *not Christian evangelism.* To use a secular phrase, we become guilty of pure, unadulterated false advertising! There is no way we can point to the evangelion, the Good News of Jesus Christ, unless our point of departure includes the Jesus Christ who associated with and healed all manner of sin, who used Samaritans as hero examples in his stories of God's unmerited grace, who broke every rabbinic tradition by treating the Samaritan woman as a human being, and who equated our relationship with the hungry and the thirsty with our relationship to himself.

I have been trying to say that our evangelism must be correlative to the evangel itself. We do this truth not only by pointing to the whole gospel through our exhortation, edification, and enlistment evangelism, but also *through the acts and deeds* of the People of God. Ethical evangelism is holding before ourselves and others the whole gospel and acting out the gospel in the world. Many Christians have regarded their most convincing evangelism to be their witness for peace, fair housing, economic justice, and human dignity.

Akin to what I am saying is what George G. Hunter, III, has called ''A New Model for Christian Witnessing.''[5] The old model, he says, followed a deductive approach in which the proclamation of a general Gospel would hopefully bring about a deduction of particular commitments of Christian service. Today, however, confession of faith has too seldom led to commitment on issues of poverty, race, pollution, and war. People are more likely to think inductively in our time, Hunter maintains, so that pragmatically an inductive witnessing method is more likely to happen than a deductive one.

Inductive evangelism, then, is most likely to occur when persons are invited to join the work of Jesus Christ in the world through commitment in a particular cause or issue with a group of Christians. With this Christological interpretation, a taste of God's kingdom is experienced, providing the basis for a commitment for all of life in the sense of scope and time. In other words the confession of Christ as Lord begins with the practice of faith in action, and is then enlarged by embracing the church's means of grace (worship, sacraments, prayer, Scripture, etc.), which sustain, nurture, and provide direction to the mission in the world.

The integrity of the Christian gospel has come alive for countless persons because they observed Christians putting their lives on the line for the powerless and those in special need. In Latin America today increasing numbers of Roman Catholic priests are facing suffering and death as a price for their commitment to justice and human dignity. Within the brief span of a single decade their deeds are dramatically reversing a centuries-old monolithic alignment of the Roman Catholic church with the privileged few. Their lives, and in many cases their deaths, are bearing witness to the gospel of release to the captives and liberty to the oppressed. The church will not be the same. The world will not be the same. This is evangelism in its deepest and purest sense.

Not everyone who says, "Lord, Lord," shall enter the kingdom of Heaven, but those who *do* God's will. Our churches have been full of people who resisted the most elementary claims of minority people for human dignity and civil liberties. Where was ethical evangelism? Ninety percent of the population in Nazi Germany was baptized and confirmed. Had evangelism taken place? Dr. Hedley Plunkett, the president of the Methodist Church in Ireland, was quoted in the *United Methodist Reporter* as saying, "Ireland has more church buildings per square mile than any other country under heaven. Somehow we failed to make our people understand that the Christian response is not merely a verbal response."[6] Ponder Helmut Gollwitzer's sobering reminder that "we belong to that third of humanity which is concerned with slimming cures, while the other two thirds are concerned with hunger. And this third consists for the most part of baptized Christians, the other two thirds of unbaptized persons."[7]

No matter how many new members may be enlisted, we will need to question whether Christian evangelism is taking place unless (1) an outline of the whole gospel, including Jesus' identification with the poor and powerless, is held before the prospective church member so that a valid initial decision may be made from which further growth can be anticipated, (2) the church struggles with the claim of the gospel to be in the midst of the great issues of our time under the Lordship of Jesus Christ. "Evangelism barely begins with conversion and profession of faith; it must always lead beyond to a lifelong mission of witness and service in the world for which Christ died."[8]

If this description of Christian evangelism is adequate in its basic design, who among us cannot get excited about evangelism? Evangelism is the total *wordeed* of the Christian community, by which the Body of Christ participates in the liberating work of God in history, both in its redemptive and emancipating features. Evangelism is that witnessing of the church to the Good News of the God of Liberation.

Enlistment Evangelism. Only when we have reviewed a panoramic view of evangelism are we ready to consider enlistment evangelism. Sometimes it is called membership visitation, outreach evangelism, or membership evangelism. Essentially it is the task of inviting others to participate in the total evangelism of the Christian church through a particular congregation. According to the circumstances, either a confession of faith or a transfer of membership from another congregation may be involved. As I have indicated, enlistment evangelism is false advertising if it invites people into an escape from the world. To be true to its own source and life, enlistment evangelism should attempt "to tell the whole story" in at least broad outline so that commitment is not falsified at the outset. This attempt is not the establishment of a legalistic standard nor a denial that discipleship means growth. To the contrary, such an effort is to suggest the New Testament truth toward which discipleship is to move and mature.

Enlistment evangelism occurs in a variety of settings. Both clergy and laity can be involved in this inviting and interpretive function by which a relationship may be established between congregation and a family or individual. It can take place at the church building, in the home, at work or elsewhere. As I have indicated, I have found it helpful for the congregation to have prepared written material which attempts to provide at least a sketch of the congregation's understanding of the gospel and some of the kinds of issues and priorities which are thereby suggested.

To believe in the evangelion is to establish an intentional ministry of visitation, invitation, and follow-up. There will be only a few who will make this commitment and stay with it, even with training and support. Enlistment evangelism is the connection with and the servant of the total evangelism of the congregation, and is thus indispensable.

I see no problem with an intentional commitment to make a specified number of calls, somewhat like the discipline of setting a deadline for a manuscript or some other project. What I think is objectionable on biblical grounds is establishing a goal for the number of persons to be "successfully evangelized" or churched for the coming year or campaign. As soon as we establish such a goal, we have made people a means to an end and have predetermined the results which we expect of the Holy Spirit. We can set goals for our *efforts* as a discipline of the faith. To set advance goals for the *results* is to manipulate people and to tempt ourselves into an evangelism of expediency. An evangelism that does not remember the rich young ruler and the many others who turned away from Jesus will become little more than a watered down commercial for institutional survival and respectability.

Guidelines for Evangelism

Having suggested what I believe is a New Testament view of evangelism, with particular attention to ethical evangelism, I propose to offer some guidelines that further connect evangelism and the concerns of liberation theologies.

1. *There is no contradiction in the biblical witness between loving a person's soul or spirit on the one hand, and caring for the human body on the other. In fact there is a compatible unity in the two.* God's love is directed toward the whole person, as is clearly evidenced in the prophetic teachings and in the teachings and example of Jesus. Consider the Parable of the Good Samaritan (Luke 10) and the Parable of the Last Judgment (Matt. 25). The healings by Jesus are acts by which human beings are made whole as total persons. Because Christ was concerned for the whole person, it is a grave contradiction to proclaim God's love, yet have little or no concern for unemployment, miserable living conditions, exploitation of persons, and other dehumanizing conditions. Therefore, evangelism and liberation are not antagonists when viewed from a biblical standpoint. They are collaborators in the total action of God in history.

It is likewise a grave error to assume that when people have obtained sound living conditions and adequate jobs that abundant life is thereby guaranteed. If this were so, the affluent sector of America would be a paradise on earth instead of a confused, defensive society oriented toward violence, drugs, and acquisitiveness. We do not live by bread alone, either in a material sense or otherwise.

Someone put the issue in perspective by saying that a church interested only in the spiritual is like a ghost and the one that is interested only in physical needs is like a cadaver. But we are called to be a living body—the Body of Jesus Christ, the Word Who Became Flesh.[9]

2. *There is no contradiction in the biblical witness between love for individuals and love or justice for society. Again, a compatible unity is evident in both Old and New Testament.* The *intention* of God's love and thus of Christian love is more significant for us today than the specific historical or cultural context of the New Testament. The shape of Christian love is not bound to a first-century world situation. Love must be imaginatively and faithfully applied in each stage of history and within the context of a given culture. To say that love must be applied or not applied today as it was or was not in the New Testament world is analogous to saying that the Lord's Supper must in our day and time take place in an upper room, and for male Jews only! Again, the content and intention of Christian love should gain our attention, not the fact that today's principalities and powers frequently appear in historical forms different than the New Testament ones.

As suggested in Chapter Two, the Old Testament prophets are clearly advocates for social justice in the name of God. The social context to which they spoke more closely resembled our own in the United States today than the New Testament conditions faced by Jesus. The prophets frequently addressed their message to the prevailing or normative religious faith within Israel at a time of great social injustices. Jesus spoke within the milieu of an occupied country, dominated by Rome, and the New Testament writers spoke to a small minority within a system of alien political and military control. Furthermore, most of the Christian minority were not persons of political, economic, or social status within the existing society.

Today we encounter enormous issues that were unheard of in New Testament times: nuclear power, ecological imbalance, pollution, medical and scientific discoveries, to name a few. As the interdependence of human beings increases in our urban, technological civilization, the responsibility for dealing with the social sources of misery and the social or corporate character and consequences of human sin becomes essential. Victor Furnish has captured this truth well in this statement:

> Because of its particularized eschatological expectation and social position, the earliest church was not required and in fact was unable to apply the love command in ways relevant to the existing social, political, and economic structures. But in principle, because the love command summons *community* into being, its call to reconciliation is no different where social institutions are involved than where it is a matter of individuals only. Oscar Cullmann is quite correct in pointing out that "as soon as centuries are reckoned with, it must necessarily be acknowledged that more just social structures also promote the individual change of character required by Jesus. A reciprocal action is therefore required between the conversion of the individual and the reform of the structures." . . . I believe we should go even farther than this and, in view of the nature of love's claim, insist that love is *only* authentic where it awakens the individual to the fact of his responsibilities within the whole complex web of interpersonal and interinstitutional relationships within which he is called to be obedient.[10]

In *The Radical Imperative* John C. Bennett has further contributed to our thought in this connection:

> We should recognize the differences between our situation and that of Jesus and the New Testament writers. The people of the New

Testament had no political power, no chance to influence public opinion in order to bring about structural changes in society. Also, they did not think in terms of an indefinite future. Planning for the future and long term struggles for social changes were out of the question, as was the use of political power.[11]

3. *The Lordship of Jesus Christ over life and history cannot be divided into secular or sacred. Jesus is Lord of all or not at all.* Both by God's love expressed through creation and by the incarnational representation of that love through Jesus Christ, we as Christians are led to affirm that no part of life can be separated from God's loving concern, presence, and action. Thus, the Christian faith has to do with power and politics as much as prayer and piety.

The Exodus is one of the great acts of God as cherished in the biblical tradition. The Hebrew slaves were emancipated from bondage and set free for a new future. If we could have interviewed Pharaoh at the time, he would have said that Moses should stick to religion and stay out of politics. Pharaoh would have seen the issue as one of power, and thus as an economic and/or political issue since his government was built on the backs of slave labor. God saw it as a *human and moral issue* and commissioned Moses, the stuttering fugitive wanted for murder in Egypt, as the instrument of liberation.

Christians such as John Wesley, William Wilberforce, and John Woolman spoke and acted against the slavery of their time in England and America. To them slavery was a human and ethical issue, and the Lordship of Jesus Christ knew no "out of bounds." From the standpoint of the slave owners, these Christians were meddling in economic and political issues. Liberation theologies have rightfully insisted that we "get back to the Bible" in the sense that God is God over all creation and Jesus Christ is Lord of all life, without exception.

4. *Active love and good will toward others in their concrete need is the only test of faith and of authentic life according to the New Testament.* This truth keeps evangelism pointed toward God's love in the world, reminding the church that participation in God's love is our reason for being. Love is the fulfillment of the law, and is that which finally measures our response to God's agape, as made clear in the Parable of the Last Judgment (Matt. 25). In Galatians Paul insists that neither circumcision nor uncircumcision counts for *anything*, but faith working through love. Church attendance, the sacraments, cultic acts, various forms of piety— all these can be means of grace that point us and others to the love of God and neighbor. They can never be tests of righteousness or proof of virtue.

5. *Love pre-supposes empowerment of the other to become his or her most true and free self for others.* Jesus' ministry was basically the empowerment of others to live their lives in freedom and dignity as children of God. Sight for the blind meant new empowerment, freedom, and responsibility. The lame and the sick made whole meant deliverance from debilitating restraints and at the same time capacity for a life of participation and accountability. Love issues forth in liberation rather than paternalistic manipulation or control. As the Good News for some brings about deliverance and empowerment, it will seem like bad news to those whose affluence and advantages were based on exploitation within inhumane systems. But as the old systems collapse the oppressors are confronted with a new future: a future no longer dependent on the servility and submissiveness of others, and thus a future with a new relationship to God, self, and neighbor.

6. *Evangelism does not introduce God to the world nor bring Christ to it; evangelism joins Christ in the work of God already underway.* The Word of God in judgment/mercy is always out before us in the life of the world. God's love was given in and through creation, and re-presented in the law, the prophets, and decisively in Jesus Christ. Evangelism is discerning, exposing, and pointing to the grace of God which preceded us in the world and which will likewise postdate us in the world.

Whenever the church deceives itself into thinking that it possesses God's Word, evangelism becomes an invitation to self-righteousness, no matter how humbly disguised. Evangelism in this vein becomes church-centered, as though Christ died for the church instead of for the world. We cannot bring Christ to the world as though he were locked up in our sanctuarial vault. We can, however, be a sign that points to God in the world.

7. *The story that evangelism has to tell is more and greater than my story.* Within the past few years the label "autobiographical theology" has become popular, at least with some. While theologizing from a personal perspective may be a needed corrective for impersonal, logical systems revealing no human struggle on the part of the theologian, the church had best not forget that our story is a tale of many centuries, a saga of many people and places, a drama of incredible variety, and most of all, a narrative of what God has done and is doing on a global and universal scene.

Any authentic version of the gospel will have a place for personal experience. I would not even know how to begin to preach without the inclusion of the personal dimension. Our tendency, however, is to reduce the gospel to the boundaries of our own experience. When this happens, evangelism is alienated from the work of God in the lives of those whose history and experience is unlike our own. The result is a tragic tunnel vision by which we become insulated from global consciousness. Evangelism's story is not just my story, but God's story for us all.

It is the story of God's free grace that is also always God's costly grace, a grace that saves us by sending us into the world for God, for others, and when all is said and done, for our own salvation. The promise/demand of costly free grace is the intersection of salvation and liberation.

CHAPTER SEVEN

Liberation Liturgy as the Work of the People

In this section we have been exploring the implications of a liberation theology for privileged and prosperous Christians. Because worship is so basic to the life of the Christian community, our exploration now needs to consider what impact a liberation theology might have on our theology and practice of worship. What I want to say can best be introduced by utilizing the term "liturgy as the work of the people." I will be laying a foundation in the initial parts of the chapter prior to the sections that deal specifically with liberation liturgy.

Participation as the Work of the People

During most of my years in the pastoral ministry I had a singular understanding of liturgy as the work of the people. If you had asked me to explain its meaning, I would have replied that the congregation's participation in the act of worship is the historical meaning of liturgy as the work of the people. This answer reflects the most widespread usage of the phrase and one that is historically sound.

The precise derivation of the term "liturgy as the work of the people" seems obscure, though it is clear that in the New Testament church, worship is a lively, active experience shared by the people. There seems to be common agreement that the Greek term *leitourgia*, from which comes our term "liturgy," means "service" or "work of the people." "The Greek term *leitourgia* refers to the performance of a public task imposed upon all who were citizens of Athens. . . . Basically, the term derives from two Greek words—the word *leitos*, meaning people, and the term *ergon*, meaning work. In the Christian Church the same concept remained, only the liturgy was the work of a new people, the people of God. To be a Christian implied doing this *leitourgia*."[1]

Liturgy as the work or active participation of the people in the service of worship is particularly identified in our thinking about the Protestant Reformation. To be sure the active involvement of the people was nothing new when compared to New Testament worship. Furthermore, the specifics of participation during the Protestant Reformation varied from reformer to reformer and came in fits and starts from place to place. Generally speaking, however, the result of the sixteenth-century reform included liturgy in the people's language, the altar table closer to the people, participation in both Eucharistic elements, the singing of hymns, the use of congregational prayers, and a greater emphasis on the preaching of the Word.

These changes in worship from the practices of the Roman Catholic church at that time reflected the Protestant concept of the church as the whole people of God. Luther in particular emphasized the priesthood of all believers, a rediscovery of the New Testament insistence that clergy and laity were all ministers to each other. Thus, the worship of the faithful was reclaimed for all the people who were to perform their work together.

I have said that liturgy as the work of the people means the active participation of the people in the act of worship. A liturgical service, then, is one in which the people are active in their worship of God. By contrast a "nonliturgical" service would be one in which the people do not actively participate, that is, they are more like spectators than participants. The distinction between the participant and the spectator, however, is not necessarily as sharp as we have often presupposed.

In human relationships and in counseling we place—or should place—a high priority on alert, aware, and creative listening. In this capacity listening is thought of as active participation. On the other hand, audible or visible forms of participation may in fact be routine and sterile. Paul Hoon in *The Integrity of Worship* reminds us that "authentic action is as much inward as outward, subconscious as conscious, attitude as well as behavior."[2] The passive action of the Quakers' meeting may involve the work of worship more geniunely than visible and audible "going through the motions."

Not long ago I was forcefully reminded of the thin difference between what we usually call participation and what we think of as being a spectator. The occasion was an Advent service of worship in the Roman Catholic parish church of Partenkirchen, West Germany.[3] As I listened to the pastor's Advent sermon in German—with the German word for "Christ" almost the only term I recognized throughout—I was impressed in a fresh way with the significance of language. How can one worship in any meaningful way with total strangers and without a speaking or hearing knowledge of the language of the service?

Yet I also began to realize that language was almost the only non-universal form of communication, and that I was indeed experiencing the worship of God. The visual and other means of worship were universal, or at least common to my own experience. There was the Advent wreath with one of its four candles burning brightly. Purple was evident in the priest's vestments and in the pulpit adornment. The music of the organ transcended the nationality of language in the spoken word. The lifting up of the wafer and the chalice bespoke of the divine presence, calling forth a tradition of the church that points to the ultimate and the universal.

In spite of distance, strangeness of place, and language barrier, the true and lively Word was made known anew to me. The richness of the church's treasury of worship/communication forms is itself an adventure—color, visual arts, familiar symbols, music, and, not least of all, the witness of the gathered people of God.

Of course the novelty of the above situation would soon wear off, if repeated again and again, and I would yearn for my own language and other factors that would enable me to participate more actively in the work of the people. But the experience was an unforgettable reminder to me that we often make definitions of participation that are doubtful. In whatever way we do define the participation of the people, that participation is one sound and substantial way of understanding liturgy as the work of the people.

Planning and Preparation as the Work of the People

During the 1960s and early 1970s a second understanding of liturgy as the work of the people surfaced in the church. In numerous congregations of various Protestant traditions, as well as the Roman Catholic church, a proliferation of worship committees or task forces emerged. The people were getting into the act of worship, not only by participation during the time of actual worship, but also by the planning and preparation of the worship itself. Liturgy became the work of the people as the people worked out the prayers, the calls to worship, and visual arts such as banners. Committees also frequently worked with the clergyperson in the preparation of the sermon. Thus, liturgy as the work of the people *preceded* the act of worship and helped to shape the liturgy in which the people would then participate.

The involvement of lay persons in planning and preparing worship is a recognition of the priesthood of all believers. Their involvement is likewise an expression of the participatory democracy and pluralism of church and society that tend to characterize our present time. If liturgy is to connect with the real-life experience of people rather than consisting of a hand-me-down printed form mimeographed in the church office, the people's planning and preparation would seem to be of paramount importance.

Today the pastor is frequently related to the worship service as liturgical director or equipper of the laity in their liturgical ministry, as one who coordinates the gifts and graces of lay persons who are preparing liturgy as their work. Speaking of the recent emphasis on the pastor's liturgical function, James F. White writes,

> Instead of simply pecking out on the typewriter, in the privacy of the study, the weekly bulletin, prayers, and sermon, the minister spent more and more time on the telephone making sure each one had prepared his or her contribution for the service. A pastor relying only on his or her own imagination became just as out of place as the preacher who never checks a commentary to benefit from other people's interpretations of scripture.[4]

Liturgy as planning and preparatory work occurs in a variety of means and methods. Some committees meet weekly with the pastor to do the work of planning each part of the service. Other committees have more limited tasks such as pre-sermon dialogue, visual arts, or the writing of prayers. These tasks reflect the experiences, the needs, and the hopes of the people in the light of the gospel. There are seasonal task groups that specialize in special services and/or in certain services such as Christmas and Easter.[5]

The participation of the laity in liturgical ministry is recognized in increasing numbers of congregations, and by academic scholars who specialize in the discipline of worship. Remarking about "The Nature of Liturgical Action," Paul Hoon has this to say: "The concept of the priesthood of all believers will come alive when liturgy is the people's work not only in the sense that they perform the action of worship, but also in the sense that they do the work of studying and planning for worship as well."[6]

Presence and Practice as the Work of the People

While the two above concepts of liturgy as the work of the people seem to be the ones mainly recognized by most Christians, there is a third viewpoint that deserves our attention. In a conversation some time ago, a Lutheran pastor suggested to me that neither of the above interpretations went to the heart of the matter as he understood it from his tradition. As the work of the people, he said, liturgy is that understanding of life vis-à-vis the Christian gospel that the people are to work out in their lives in the world. To be sure the people's participation in the cultic service of worship is a liturgical act or work, but the essential point of the liturgy is that it be worked out *in the world* in the priesthood of all believers.

I hope you can get as excited as I about this third interpretation of liturgy as the work of the people, that is, as the *presence* in the world of the priesthood of all believers and as the *practice* of the liturgy in the life of the world. In one sense there is nothing new about this notion because Christian worship has always had to do with the way the church goes about its work in the world. Yet the notion of liturgy as the work of the people being the *practice* of the liturgy in the world provides a handle for communicating the enormous importance of Christian liturgy. This notion is increasingly recognized and expounded by a number of Third World theologians. The whole liturgical orbit looks like this:

Liturgy as the Work of the People

Before the Cultic Act of Worship	Planning/Preparation
During the Cultic Act of Worship	Participation/Performance
After the Cultic Act of Worship	Presence/Practice

The practice of liturgy in life means that the liturgy of the cultic act, or worship service as we call it, becomes the *script,* the *story* out of which I am called to live my life as a member of the Body of Christ in the world. The liturgy is not merely a routine corporate form or an individual-istic expression at the morning hour on the Lord's Day. The liturgy—whatever its form and shape—is that which communicates my identity as a Christian. My liturgical work as a Christian, whether lay or clergy, is to live out the content of the liturgy because that content is the description of my life's meaning. Seen from that vantage point, liturgy is "the stuff" of our life before God and neighbor in the world.

The Liturgy-Life Connection

The content of Christian liturgy offers the shape of our response to God's gift of life from day to day, that is, our work as the People of God in the world. Because of this I have come to appreciate a recurring liturgical content. While one has to be cautious about insisting on a definitive itemizing or categorizing of worship content, it is also true that we do not stand before just any god in general. Indeed, our worship content as Christians can do no other than to portray and represent the ultimate, universal, and underlying promise and claim of God's everlasting and unconditional love in Jesus Christ.

When we speak of liturgy as the work of the people in the sense that it is the people's script for life—and thus for service or mission in the world—we are suggesting neither a work's righteousness nor an imperative without grace. Insofar as any Christian responds in faith to God's gift of life, it is a response called into being, nurtured, and empowered by the grace of God. Christian worship is first and last about what God has done, is doing, and will do. It is only because that is so that we can even speak of the work of God's people in the world.

What, then, are some primary themes or motifs in Christian liturgy that constitute our work in the world? In church history there have been innumerable variables of forms within two basic types of liturgical framework: the Eucharistic Service, also known as the Lord's Supper or Holy Communion; and the non-eucharistic Sunday morning service, which, as James F. White reminds us, has never received a commonly accepted name and thus may simply be called the Sunday Service.[7]

Since at least the second century, the Eucharistic Service has included ingredients of the Sunday Service, followed by a fourfold pattern of the Eucharist. The fourfold order, outlined by Dom Gregory Dix in *The Shape of the Liturgy*,[8] as well as other scholars and students of Christian liturgy, consists of the taking of bread and cup (preparation), the blessing or expression of thanks, the breaking of bread, and the giving of the bread and the cup. As already indicated, this structure supports many variables of style and manner of expression.

How does the eucharistic liturgy inform our work in the world? Or more to the point, how does it become the script or model for our life in the world? First of all, the Eucharist focuses initially not on what we are to do, but what God has done for us. The unconditional gift of God's love, that is, God's own being or self, is dramatized in visible manner through the Eucharist. This gift constitutes the first and last Word about life to the Christian and is the root or foundation of all action in the world. God's love, re-presented in the Eucharist, is the source and end of our lives, and thus the only framework for our life in the world.

The eucharistic action lays before us, as does any and all authentic Christian liturgy, that ultimate and universal promise of God's love in the light of which all other promises must be seen and weighed—the promise of the state, the family, the economic system, to name a few. Our work in the world cannot be God's work if any other promise is allowed to become "the promise" of life. In Christian theology, of course, the substitution of any other promise for God's promise is known as idolatry.

The Eucharist also "sets forward the redemptive work of Christ in us, enabling us as the Body of Christ to become what by his act he has made us."[9] Christ's act is one of sacrifice and self-giving, thus pointing to "how his life was to be taken and consecrated, broken and poured out for the world."[10] The act of Christ is to be our act in the world. It is this liturgical content that is to be our work in the world. The imperative "do this" proceeds from the indicative "this is my body and blood given for you." From the ultimate promise to us comes forth the ultimate claim on us, namely, the claim of God through Christ to join God's action in the world.

Liturgy's connection with life is more than confrontation and decision on Sunday morning. Certainly the cultic or congregational gathering is a time when the history of God's acts are rehearsed, re-presented, and re-appropriated, encompassing both Old and New Covenants. Past events intersect with the present, so that the worshipper is once again confronted with God's saving grace and the decisions for which it calls. As the liturgy is enacted on Sunday morning again and again, it becomes part of the formation of our selfhood rather than merely a Sunday action. Thus as the eucharistic action informs and transforms our self-understanding, our value system, our way of looking at and responding to life, it becomes part of our identity. This is a life-long process that shapes our personal history.

To say it another way, we discern the Word of God as it meets us in the world by rehearsing and re-hearing the Word of God in Jesus Christ in the gathered congregation. In the ordinary events of life we encounter the same Word of God that is proclaimed and remembered and dramatized in the cultic act of worship. Liturgy as the work of the people is that link between the Word in worship and the Word in the world.

Through the years it has been pointed out by liturgical scholars that liturgy is the theology of the laity, the chief school of faith, the great lay catechism. Liturgy carries the history of salvation, and when that history becomes our history, life is never the same again because the lens through which we perceive life, live life, and anticipate life is the aperture of the gospel.

The second basic form of Christian worship is the non-eucharistic Sunday morning service. During the past twenty years the structure of service with which I have most frequently worshipped has been a sequence of confession, praise/celebration, offering/commitment. Realizing that neat distinctions cannot easily be made between praise and confession and commitment, I nevertheless have come to experience the structure as a valid description of the God of Jesus Christ and our relationship to God.

I do not go as far as some Christians who claim that this threefold division is "the common structure behind the varied structures of Christian worship."[11] I do think that these three expressions of worship are basic to the Christian understanding of life, that they do accurately and adequately tell much of the life story of the person who stands before God in Christ, that Christian worship is impoverished without these dimensions, and that the threefold structure is as close to an authentic consensus as might be found in the complexities of liturgical history. Let us look briefly at each of the three as part of our work in the world.

Confession. Our worship of God stands on the recognition that God-in-Christ is the One before whose promise and claim we live our lives and die our deaths. Christian confession is the work by which we acknowledge the sovereignty of God over all of life; it is this One with whom we have to do for our past, present, and future. Accordingly, confession is also a sign that no entity or reality in this world finally holds our life or can either give or take away our true life before God. Through confession we recognize that we are not to be conformed to this world, but transformed by the transcendent power of God. The Lord of Lords is not the state, the economic system, the opinion of others, nor our status before present powers and principalities.

Because confession is based on the belief and the experience that God's love can change our lives, it is an affirmation of the self. Those who have maintained that confession is a form of self-negation have not understood the powerful dynamic of opening ourselves to God's transforming gift of unmerited love. Our openness to God's love through confession does not earn God's love. It is God's love, or prevenient grace, as Wesley called it, that enables us to respond with a "yes" to God's initiating love. Through this response God frees us from our past for a new future. Thus, Christian confession is an act of faith in God's love and is thereby a posture of hope toward the future that God brings. Otherwise it becomes a humanistic focus on our own condition instead of God's grace.

Confession is the recognition that when human beings lose the capacity for self-examination and repentance in the light of God's disturbing-healing love, our future is already sealed in the past. One cannot easily forget the radical honesty in an Alcoholics Anonymous meeting: "My name is ——— and I'm an alcoholic." This is the gateway to change and without it there is no hope. The honest recognition and awareness of one's condition is the beginning of health. It is this truth about life to which Christian confession points.

Far from providing a crutch for those who seek flight from scrutiny of self, or from adult responsibilities in a complex world, confession as held before us in Christian liturgy involves us in a perspective representing the ultimate maturity for humanity. We are reminded that in order to truly live life, we must "die" again and again to our tendency to be prisoners or victims of life who are content to be *less* than we were created to be, or else pretenders who insist on being *more* than we were created to be. Confession, then, is a life posture or style, not simply a printed or extemporaneous prayer in the Sunday order of worship. The intent of a confessional prayer is to experience the reality of confession in that moment and to implant in our life posture an openness to truth as a way of life.

Celebration, Praise, Thanksgiving. The Christian faith was born in the grave. Because God is forever making new beginnings out of life's endings, because God is endlessly emptying into life the Word of love that we might be full, because God rules the world with truth and grace as the suffering/sovereign One of history, because God makes something out of nothing, because God's irrepressible grace through a crucified Savior enables us to live our lives in spite of all the in spite ofs—the Christian life is eucharistic!

Christian celebration is not a denial of death, the suffering of the world, or the tragic dimensions of life. Christian joy is an affirmation that God made the world out of crucifixion/resurrection. To say this is to affirm that life's meaning does not finally rest in either the power of evil or in our best efforts to make the world "work," but in God's before-us and after-us love by which all things are called into being and by which they are everlastingly embraced for what they are.

Although I cannot recall the exact time or place, I can distinctly recall the empowering release that came to me when I first deeply realized the Christian gospel is truth about human existence that needs no reward other than its own truth and beauty. My friend Jane Marshall has superbly set this fact to music in her anthem, "My Eternal King":

My God, I love Thee;
not because I hope for heaven thereby,
 nor yet because who love Thee not must die eternally.
Thou, O my Jesus,
Thou didst me upon the cross embrace;
For me didst bear the nails and spear and manifold disgrace;
Why, then, why, O blessed Jesus Christ,

should I not love Thee well?
Not for hope of winning heaven, or of escaping hell;
Not with the hope of gaining aught, not seeking a reward;
But as Thyself hast loved me, O ever loving Lord!
E'en so I love Thee, and will love, and in Thy praise will sing;
Solely because Thou art my God and my Eternal King.[12]

When liturgy expresses the heart of life as thanksgiving for life and joy in life as God's good gift, it is expressing more than a momentary feeling or act in the service of worship. It is holding before us a picture of our identity as justified through God's grace and thus reminds us of what God has done and is doing in the world. The Christian story is one of praise, joy, and gratitude, a celebration that may be experienced through the sermon, prayers, and hymns of thanksgiving, an affirmation of faith, and other expressions of worship.

Commitment, Offering, Sacrifice. Where there is grace, there is responsibility. It is fitting that Christian worship moves through confession to praise for God's acts of redemption to the renewal of God's mission in the world. This third portion of the worship reminds us that Christian life is not a special privilege but a called responsibility.

In the memorable passage Isaiah 6:1-8, which depicts the prophet's ecstatic vision of God in the temple, the awestruck Isaiah experiences the utter holiness of God's presence. Out of this sense of God's majesty and otherness comes Isaiah's confession: "Woe is me! For I am lost; for I am a man of unclean lips . . ." (v. 5). His experience of repentance is followed by a cleansing forgiveness: ". . . your guilt is taken away, and your sin forgiven" (v. 7). In the very next verse the voice of the Lord says, "Whom shall I send, and who will go for us?" And Isaiah responds, "Here I am! Send me!" (v. 8).

To be touched with God's burning coal (vv. 6-7) is not merely a cancelling of guilt, nor a theoretical exercise in forgiveness. Forgiveness implies a new future in God's service, that is, obedience to a new covenant and commitment to a new claim. To be justified, forgiven, or saved is to be sent. To be redeemed is to be called into the hallowing of life through God's work in the world. Christian liturgy points us in this direction. In response to God's grace, our liturgy as the work of the People of God is to bend and expend ourselves for others as did the Pioneer and Perfecter of our faith.

Having worshipped for a number of years utilizing the movement of confession, praise, and commitment, I can say that my identity or formation as a Christian has been significantly shaped in the process. The liturgy has become my story, my tradition, my script for responding to

God's initiative. Liturgy reminds us of what faith looks like in our personal and corporate lives. Of course the order of worship may vary greatly, and today we are seeing acts of confession frequently placed after the proclamation of the Word.

It is worth noting, however, that the threefold structure outlined above pulsates with the movement of the Christian year, or at least one understanding of that year. As Advent—Christmas—Epiphany calls us from penitence and anticipation to joyous victory and affirmation to responsibility in the world, so it is with the rhythm of the Christian liturgy I have been describing. The cycle repeats itself from Lent to Easter to Pentecost. The pulsebeat of our life in daily work, in recreation and leisure, in the political and economic realm, and in the family sphere is that of Christian liturgy. If our script is not from the Christian year, then we will live from some other script or story—such as the liturgy of the state, the corporation, or personal aggrandizement.

The New Testament proclaims a clear connection between liturgy and life or cultus and mission. Since the Greek word for liturgy, as we have seen, indicates the work of the people, liturgy applies to the totality of life. For this reason New Testament worship refers to the Christian's total existence.

> Our traditional understanding of worship as restricted to the cultic gathering of the congregation at a designated time and place for rite and proclamation will no longer do. This is not what the New Testament means by worship. . . . The life and work of Christ are biblically understood in terms of both worship and mission, and cultic terms are interchangeably employed (especially by Paul) to apply to the totality of life, not merely to gathering for rite and cult. . . .
>
> In short, the thrust of our recovered understanding of the New Testament conception of worship moves us to a view of the Christian's life in its totality as a liturgical life, and in exploring this profound meaning lies the clue to overcoming the gulf between the Church's worship and the life her laity live in the world. . . .[13]
>
> The New Testament conception of worship as the unity of leitourgia and diakonia, of worship and service, must always be borne in mind.[14]

Now we are at the point of examining a further linkage: the connection between liberation theology for the privileged and prosperous, and liturgy as the work of the people.

Liberation Liturgy as the Work of the People

In speaking of liberation liturgy I am thinking of a liturgy that interprets liberation in its holistic sense of redemption and emancipation as suggested in the Appendix. The weakness of too much of our liturgy is that it has short-changed the whole gospel into a privatistic "me-and-my-God" religion. While liturgy inevitably addresses the individual life of the worshipper, it is primarily the work of the corporate Body of Christ as contrasted with personal devotions and spirituality.[15] The liturgical life of the Christian in the New Testament is an expression of the whole people of God in their social holiness or corporate mission in the world.

A liturgy that faithfully freights the Gospel and calls us to our liturgical work in the arenas of life will be global in its consciousness, aware of the suffering of the wretched of the world, and throbbing with the imagery of God's foolishness (Chapter Two). The noise of solemn assemblies must become the noise of intentional social responsibility. When this happens the church's liturgy nourishes and reinforces the personal interiority or spirituality of the individual worshipper. But this spirituality is not an escape from the world's suffering; it is a faith where spirit and flesh become one.

Liberation liturgy as the work of the people is no stranger in existing liberation theologies nor in the liturgical communities they represent. The worship of the black community, for example, has historically spelled out "the story" for minority survival and hope amid suffering. In oppressed communities of Latin America the liturgy of the church is increasingly the liturgy of the people by which the process of conscientization is implemented. The Golconda movement in Colombia has used the church's liturgy as the prime vehicle of a new awareness as subjects of history rather than objects. Participation in the liturgy calls for a community dedicated to building a society of justice and love for all.

Existing Liturgies: Interpreting the Implications

The development of a liberation liturgy among privileged and prosperous Christians will require two types of effort. The first is to interpret the implications of the liturgies already in use. Our present baptism rituals, with one conspicuous exception to be noted presently, are clear refutations of racism and sexism because they express the universality of God's grace and thus of inclusion in the family of Christ. Throughout most of our sacramental liturgies the redemptive grace of God is a powerful force for human liberation in the sense that it is unconditional, unmerited, and universal in its implications. As liturgical theologians, pastors need to *interpret* these implications so that worshippers are aware of them.

There is no better example than the Eucharist itself. Increasing numbers of Christians are becoming acutely—and sometimes painfully— aware that to share in the Universal Body of Christ is more than an ecclesiastical Sunday morning exercise involving crackers and crumbs. To participate in the broken loaf of our Lord's Body is to raise the question of a universal community, . . . which is to raise the question of our common humanity and thus the dilemma of the extreme disparity between the affluent and the hungry, . . . which is finally, at least in part, an economic and political matter. Inevitably, an insightful interpretation of God's universal grace—the bedrock of all Christian theology—will propel us into the midst of concern for human liberation. To make the connection between liturgy and life remains a key assignment of the pastor.

Bishop John A. T. Robinson has forcefully articulated the Eucharist as follows:

> The Eucharist is the clue to the Christian renewal of the social order. Just as this action is the pattern of all Christian action, so the society known here is the pattern of all society redeemed in Christ. The Holy Communion is the great workshop of the new world. . . . Here indeed is the classless society in which there is neither Jew nor Greek, male nor female, bond nor free. . . . The Communion is social dynamite, if we really take seriously the pattern of community known at the altar. The Church discovered that, in time, in the case of slavery. We have to discover it in terms of race and class and all that is involved for the distribution of the world's resources in the practice, in which we indulge so thoughtlessly each Sunday, of the absolutely unconditional sharing of bread.[16]

By sensitive explanation of our existing liturgies, Christian liturgists can draw out their universal implications. Some of this task can be done in preaching and some in occasional step-by-step commentary as the people participate in the Sunday morning liturgy, whether it be Scripture, prayers, calls to worship, responsive lessons, or music through anthems and hymns. If liturgy is to be the work of the people on Wednesday afternoon or Friday evening, its meaning needs to be broken open on Sunday morning with the help of the liturgical director (pastor).

Liturgical Reconstruction vis-à-vis Liberation Theology

J. G. Davies, in his book *Worship and Mission,* recounts his experience of examining the collects in the *Book of Common Prayer* with the hope of finding explicit references of worship's relation to mission. His discovery was that eighty-two out of eighty-six collects are concerned solely with the church and its members, with only four having any reference to the world.[17]

Similarly, in 1965 the *Christian Advocate* published an article of mine entitled, "Is Our Communion Liturgy Christian?," the reference being to the Methodist liturgy at that time. The thrust of the article was to deplore the near omission of reference to our neighbor, and especially the neighbor as one who is in need, who may radically offend us, and who may be radically unlike us.

> Of course we could argue that it is the task of the preached Word to carry the particularity and the contemporaneity of the Gospel's judgment-redemption. It would be wiser to suggest that the liturgical expression should be consistent with the written word (Bible) and the preached Word. To go one step further, it might also be wise to suggest that the radical explicitness and terrible specificity of the Gospel should be built into the sacramental liturgy so that the presence of the whole kerygma does not have to depend every Communion Sunday on a faithful or prophetic preacher![18]

Liturgical reconstruction has been in progress for the past dozen years or so in most Protestant communions, partly spawned by the impact of Vatican II. In some respects liturgical reform is moving in the direction of greater attention to the church's mission in the world. This direction was envisioned by Massey Shepherd, Jr., in his statement, "The liturgy exists primarily to inform a Christian's vocation in the world and to set him on fire for mission."[19]

While denominational liturgical establishments can provide some improvements in our liturgies, a great deal depends on the faithfulness of the local pastor and lay worship committee. Some examples of greater visibility for a liberation liturgy as the work of the people are suggested below:

1. *Call to Worship, Call to Prayer, and Versicles.* Calls to Worship and Calls to Prayer can utilize passages that reinforce the bond between worship and liberation, or, said otherwise, between redemption and

emancipation: 1 Corinthians 1:27-29 (God chose what is foolish . . .); Luke 4:18-19 (using portions at least and using "us" or "the church" instead of "me" to indicate that the corporate task of the church is to do the ministry of Jesus); Isaiah 2:12, 17 (The Lord of hosts has a day . . .). The Call to Worship can convey both the indication of God's initiating promise and the imperative of life with our neighbor as an indelible part of the promise.

2. *Choice of Hymns and Anthems.* An intentionality at this point can at least increase the use of hymns and anthems that deal responsibly with mission in the world as grounded in God's grace. Unfortunately, many of the "hymns for today" are little more than highly subjective "feelin' groovy" types that are testimonies to theological bankruptcy and psychological narcissism. Their older counterparts in our hymn books, while known as gospel hymns, offer only a portion of gospel almost totally divorced from any kind of task in the world, whether individual or social. Of course not every hymn can attest to both redemption and emancipation. The best for which we can hope is an intentional selectivity that tells the *whole* story in as frequent a cycle as possible.

3. *Prayers and Collects.* If written prayers of confession are used, our blindness toward the suffering of others and our complicity in their suffering through our own social and economic systems can be articulated. Similarly, prayers of commitment can outline our coming liturgical work in the world. Here are some examples I have used in Sunday morning worship, or in which I have participated.

THE PRAYER OF CONFESSION

God our Creator and Redeemer, we bring to you that which we truly are; self-centered, undisciplined, and undeserving of your constant gift of life. When life has given comfort, we have become complacent. When life has given suffering, we have become self-pitying. When life has given us new visions, we have become timid. When life has given us those in need, we have become self-protecting. Deliver us, O God, we beseech you, from our living death, and grant us the courage to accept both the joy and the pain of new birth each remaining day which is given, through Jesus Christ our Lord. Amen.

Most merciful God, we have seldom received your Kingdom in this world, fostered goodwill among enemies, or established love as the way of life. We have allowed self to blind us, pains to embitter us. We have forgotten that whatever is done to one of the least of your people is done unto you. Pardon our shortcomings; forgive our neglect; give us a pure heart intent on pleasing you. Help us in all our seeking to seek first your kingdom and your righteousness. And make us to come, as Jesus Christ came, not to be ministered unto, but to minister. All of which we ask through Jesus Christ our Lord. Amen.

Everloving God, we admit that we have thought about ourselves more than about others. We have bought lovely clothes for ourselves and have forgotten about those who must dress in rags. We live in fine houses and are not concerned about those who have no place to live. We have fed ourselves too much food and have neglected to provide for those who are starving. We have forgotten the needs of those whose economic standards did not permit them to buy the bare necessities of life. We have failed to share our plenty with those in need and we have failed to give hope through the sharing of love. O Lord, forgive. Forgive us in Christ's name. Amen.

(United Methodist Men's Retreat,
Cozad, Nebraska, 1977)

Recognizing our flight from limits, O God, we the children of affluence confess that we are deeply restless with the limits that have been placed before us. We, who would push back the frontier of space and learn the secrets of the genetic code, whose technology has promised us unlimited freedom and control over our world, and whose aspirations for the future have soared above every restraint, every resistance, every boundary; we confess that without such achievements we are rendered profoundly insecure about ourselves. We find it hard to say no to our deepest ambitions, our longing for conquest and control, for novelty and growth, for more and more of everything. Forgive us, O God, for the madness of our hearts, for those we have violated in our arrogance and anxiety about ourselves, for failing to learn reverence for our earth and respect for the logic of life. Teach us the wisdom of balance, of humility, of the graceful acceptance of the wellbeing of the whole. In the name of Jesus Christ, who taught us to lose our lives in order to find them. Amen.

(by Donald Ferrell)

THE CORPORATE INTERCESSION AND COMMITMENT

Almighty God, who waits for us in the middle of the world, already present with the neighbor whom we have judged and rejected, call us forth from the comfort of our togetherness to accept the vocation of servanthood. Sustain us to bear both our own anxieties and the anxieties of others that we might testify to the strength that is in us and in them through you. We accept our common lot with all the hungry, the frustrated, the exploited, the wounded, the isolated, and the insulted people of this world for the sake of our common redemption. This we pray in the name of the one who has already borne our griefs and shared our sorrows, Jesus Christ. Amen.

Let us pray for the people all around us whose lives are difficult and troubled and whose suffering is unseen, for those who are sad and disillusioned, and for those who can no longer find any meaning in life. Let us also pray for people who are alone in life, who cannot get through the day or find friendship anywhere. We pray, God, for all who are victims, murdered people, those who die in traffic accidents, for children who have no parents, for prisoners and strangers, for refugees without a country and without a name, for people who live in conflict with each other and who cannot find any solution to it, for those who are ill without any hope of cure. We also pray to you, God, for our dead. Remember their names and preserve their lives. Through Jesus Christ our Lord. Amen.

Lord of history, Lord of all; grant that we might discover the feast of life in fasting for others, for the sake of our common liberation. Lead us through your gift of costly free grace, that we might come to know the Christ of the poor and the powerless as our Christ. Open our eyes to the ways in which economic and social systems benefit us to the detriment of others. And most of all, O Lord, reveal to us the courage to have our lifestyles and our life systems shaped by the life, death, and resurrection of Jesus Christ. Amen.

O Suffering and Sovereign God, amidst the impoverishment of our affluence, call us to the Good Life of moving toward others in their suffering and need. If we become oblivious to the cries of the world, convict us of our low standard of living and liberate us for abundant life. If we use prayer and piety as means to avoid your claim on us, haunt and hound us with your Divine Discontent that we might become instruments of your will. Teach us again and again, O God, that it is by faith working through love that we come to know you as the source and chief end of all life. Amen.

If prayers of the people are used, the worship committee may want to take responsibility for seeing that special concerns are held before the people in prayers—flood victims, the unemployed, those in prison. In this way the *whole* world as our parish is lifted up in the name of Christ, at least in a symbolic way. The expression of concerns of the church can function in a similar way.

4. *The Benediction or Sending Forth.* This conclusion of the service is the last link between liturgy as the people's participation in the gathered congregation and liturgy as the practice of faith in the world by the scattered people. What has previously been said about the Call to Worship and the Call to Prayer applies to the sending forth of the people for their ministry of salt and leaven in the world.

5. *Sexist Language.* Earlier I stated that our existing liturgies, such as baptism rituals, refuted racism and sexism through the universalism of God's grace and of inclusion in the family of Christ. I also noted that presently I would comment on a contradiction to that universality, namely, the sexist language that tends to prevail in our liturgical language. I have placed sexist language in its own category because it pervades all the others—calls to worship, hymnody, prayers and collects, and preaching.

I'm fully aware that many Christians, lay and clergy, believe that the consternation over imagery and language is either disloyal to our biblical tradition or else a feminist fuss over trivia. I want to add my voice to those, both male and female, who believe language *is* significant in the church and in society at large.

In Chapter Four I shared in an autobiographical way something of the liberating effects of female liberation for my life as a male. As far as language is concerned, I look back on my previous use of words and am now astounded—and embarrassed—by use of what I now regard as sexist language. The power of cultural osmosis! But what difference does language make?

One does not have to be a professional linguist to become convinced that our self-image is partially determined by the cultural expectations around us. If the cultural symbols, of which language is an important part, consistently signal that male is *first* and female is *second* or derivative, the formation of the self interiorizes that value system. Although a reconstructed language cannot be a substitute for a reconstructed order of relationships, rights, and roles, language is a powerful force in reflecting and shaping life. "Language is the prime reflection of the power of the ruling group to define reality in its own terms and demote oppressed groups into invisibility. Women, more than any other group, are overwhelmed by a linguistic form that excludes them from visible existence."[20]

In liturgical language we deny the universality of God's grace and the corresponding human equality when male is exclusively associated with the supreme or ultimate value and with a so-called generic capacity that covers both sexes. To take seriously the personhood of females is to take seriously those cultural symbols that point to their existence, including pronouns.

For these reasons it is important for the church to become sensitized to language and imagery as it relates to the personhood of women. Specifically, liturgical reconstruction might include at least these two steps:

1. Well-prepared and sensitive sermon presentations on the issue of women's consciousness; prophetic preaching that combines sound biblical, theological interpretation with personal "confessions," e.g., the reality of one's own personal struggle and change.

2. Efforts in the direction of more inclusive theologizing, liturgy, and hymnody. If a worship committee can become alerted and committed to the goal of nonsexist language and women participants in the worship service, significant improvements can be initiated. While much of our liturgical language is "fixed" in terms of hymnody and regularly ordered services, such as baptism, confirmation, and the Eucharist, there is freedom to alter sexist language and/or to write new prayers and calls to worship, as mentioned above. However, a centuries-old dilemma will not be overcome by a few alternatives from the pastor's pen or by several committee meetings. But we can address the issue and begin to work together on a more inclusive terminology and thus a more Christian liturgy.

The problem of sexist language will demand a generation or more of diligent efforts. It will require more accurate translation of Hebrew and Greek texts and some head-on confrontation with key biblical images. Age-old customs will need to give way to changing language in the church. All of this will contribute, as Letty M. Russell has worded it, to liberating the Word to be the liberating Word.[21]

The Peril and the Promise of Liberation Liturgies

"Can liturgy which celebrates the lordship of Christ fail to refer to the powers of this world?"[22] To refer to powers and principalities runs the risk of politicizing the gospel into an ideology. To fail to do so runs the risk of an irrelevant, escapist liturgy that sanctions existing systemic violence, thus becoming a further instrument of oppression. A biblically sound liberation liturgy for privileged and prosperous Christians will avoid an imperative of program or project, yet call for participation in the suffering of God and humanity as the work of the people. A faithful and creative liberation liturgy will expand moral imagination, encourage movement toward others in their need, lift up faith symbols and images that focus on the remembrance of Christ's outreaching love, and point toward the kingdom of God that calls into question every form of bondage and servitude. In these ways liberation liturgy, like the God to whom it points and for whom it speaks, "takes sides"!

In an article entitled, "Lines of Political Action in Contemporary Liturgy," Herman Schmidt places the peril and the promise of political liturgies into perspective:

> The Exodus, the history of Jesus Christ, the biblical notion of God, the idea of the covenant, the shalom-idea, the kingdom of God, the vision of the new Jerusalem and above all the Cross of Christ have political dimensions but are more than patterns of mundane political action. There is an eschatological proviso attached to the biblically and politically oriented liturgy. That does not mean for the Christian, however, that he is to give politics a wide berth and be indifferent towards it. On the contrary, biblical eschatology incites us to a life of intense and sensitive "distinguishing of spirits" and requires the adoption of a standpoint, engagement and participation in the struggle.
>
> In the eschatological perspective the believer does not remain politically neutral, but is moved to empathy and summoned to take sides—but always with a reservation. The political plane is not the ultimate one. Political history is not salvation-history. Politics is linked with the last things, but is not the last things. Political action is bound up with salvation but is not the bringer of salvation.[23]

The risks of liturgy and preaching that take liberation theologies seriously cannot be avoided. In addition to other risks there is the risk of offense. As I have pointed out, liberation theology is not for anemic Christians for whom salvation is equated with either this-worldly security or otherworldly comfort. On the other hand, liturgical hat-tipping to the concerns of liberation theologies can become a theatre of substitute imagery, an artificial world of symbolic innoculation from real social and political involvement. Perhaps the greatest risk for privileged and prosperous Christians, speaking from the standpoint of our standing with the Lord of the Church and the World, is to avoid the other two risks.

Soundings on Theologies of the Oppressed

Like all other theological efforts, the content and the methods of liberation theology are subject to critical analysis. Objections to liberation theologies, or facets of them, may be on the level of theological adequacy and faithfulness. Or the objectors may resist the kinds of changes called for in the imperatives of the message itself. Sometimes complaints about these imperatives are disguised as concerns about theological adequacy. On the other hand, critics of theological adequacy may be dismissed by devotees of liberation theology as racists, chauvinists, or imperialists *because* they raise critical questions. The intention of this appendix is to review several of the most frequent criticisms of liberation theology, to offer my own ruminations on these critiques, and to challenge you to do likewise on your own terms.

Narrowness of Biblical Images Selected by Liberation Theologians

Many liberation theologians have lifted up the Exodus event in the Old Testament and the Luke 4:16-30 "rejection at Nazareth" story as *the* quintessence of Scripture. There tends to be concentration on an intimate circle of passages that have "high liberation visibility." While these passages carry their own legitimate weight, does the neglect of other biblical content skew the claims of liberation theologians to the point of a basic distortion? To raise the question in a slightly different manner, do liberation theologies tend to remake the gospel into a socio-political message first of all, and a word about the God-human relationship through Jesus Christ secondarily?

In reading the New Testament, one quickly becomes aware of a universal quality in many passages that transcends the particularities of economic, political, and cultural liberation. For example much that Jesus has to say—as we hear him through the oral tradition, the written tradition, and the evangelists of the New Testament—cuts across *all* human conditions, whether economic, political, racial, or national. He speaks of personal relationships in the light of God's judgment and grace. His words often speak of faith, forgiveness, and prayer. He heals all sorts of conditions without regard to place or status in life.

The universal quality of much of the biblical narrative bears out a claim that I made in *Christ's Suburban Body* (1970): "The peculiar temptation of a theology of social change is to concentrate on God's activity in political events to the exclusion of a personal gospel concerned with the universal human condition of guilt, anxiety, and death, and the universal human need for acceptance, joy, and understanding."[1] Not everything in the Bible can, should, or needs to be squeezed into the funnel of liberation, unless we define liberation to mean any and all implications of God's grace as it relates to the divine-human relationship on both the individual and the societal level.

Having said this, it seems equally clear that there is a recurring particularity in the New Testament which *is* concerned with the relationship between the poor and the rich, the weak and the strong, the outcast and the religiously and socially accepted. This particularity is especially apparent in the gospel of Luke, which therefore frequently receives special attention from liberation theologians. I agree with James Cone in his statement, "Maybe our white theologians are right when they insist that I have overlooked the universal significance of Jesus' message. But I contend that there is no universalism that is not particular."[2]

Whatever the biblical relationship of the universal and the particular may be, there is a consistent particularity which makes up a legitimate grounding for the claims of liberation theology. This "gestalt" is repeated again and again: warnings against the rich; cautions against unforgiving legalistic attitudes lacking in mercy and compassion; Jesus' identification with the poor through the narration of his birth, of his preaching good news to the poor, and of his associating with the outsiders of his time; and the portrayal of the early church as a community that practiced the sharing of possessions. From these passages it becomes clear that the *particularity* of which we are speaking is in fact a *partiality* on God's part, a matter about which a great deal has been said throughout this book.

Possibly the most frequent criticism of some liberation theology from a biblical and theological basis is that it tends to obscure the characteristic

New Testament emphasis, predominant as a whole in both the gospels and the Pauline letters, on the primacy of the God-human relationship. While generalizations are risky, I believe it is accurate to say that in the New Testament reconciliation and freedom customarily have to do *first* with the God-human relationship that is basic, although this relationship is integrally related to the entire range of relationships and structures, including socio-political liberation. In Jesus' message the proclamation of the kingdom of God is primary, a conviction that is shared by most New Testament theologians.

> The central aspect of the teaching of Jesus was that concerning the Kingdom of God. Of this there can be no doubt and today no scholar does, in fact, doubt it. Jesus appeared as one who proclaimed the Kingdom; all else in his message and ministry serves a function in relation to that proclamation and derives its meaning from it. (John Dominic Crossan[3])

> Repent, for the Kingdom of Heaven is at hand (Matthew 4:17). . . . With these words the first two evangelists sum up the whole message of Jesus. (Günther Bornkamm[4])

> The message of Jesus centers upon the Kingdom of God . . . altogether the three Synoptic Gospels contain approximately 114 references to the Kingdom of God. (Robert Spivey and D. Moody Smith, Jr.[5])

> The dominant concept of Jesus' message is the reign of God. The coming of God's reign is a miraculous event which will be brought by God alone without the help of men. (Rudolf Bultmann[6])

In Paul's message, too, the priority of the God-human relationship through God's initiative seems clear. If we take Romans as a substantial expression of Paul's theology, the individual's freedom from the bondage of sin, law, meaninglessness, and death through justification by God's grace is the central affirmation. For Paul the flow of the gospel is something like this: First, the initiative of God's unmerited and unbounded love as the ultimate, universal, and unifying promise and claim of human existence—given in creation yet concretized in the Old Testament covenant with Abraham, ratified through the law and the prophets, and fulfilled through Jesus Christ. Second, the human responses of faith by which God's redemptive love becomes the center of one's life as both source and end. Third, as a sound tree bears good fruit, to use Jesus' Sermon on the Mount language, the consequences of faith and freedom in God's grace as a life appropriate to that grace: namely, a life committed to freedom, justice, and dignity for all other human beings.

If the characteristic New Testament approach as a whole is described adequately above, the comment that liberation theologies come to good conclusions with inadequate arguments may be on target. The area of contention is not whether commitment to the gospel should lead to a new order of relationships, values, and priorities, including the socio-political. The questions are whether or not at least some liberation theologies define liberation in sufficiently broad terms and what constitutes the undergirding or grounding for cultural, economic, and political changes.

At this point I have found the thinking of Schubert M. Ogden to be instructive and clarifying. He claims that theologies of liberation "do not properly distinguish and relate the two essentially different though closely related forms of liberation, that is, redemption and emancipation."[7] Theologically understood, God's liberating work is first of all the *redemptive* act of freeing us from sin, law, and death (to be understood in Paul's terms) and thus for others. As this freedom for others makes itself active, we participate with God in God's *emancipating* work of liberation from sexism, racism, imperialism, and all other forms of bondage. It has been said that the decisive issue of liberation theology is the relation of Christian freedom to political liberty. To use Paul's thought in Romans again, liberation from sin, death, law, and the demonic (that is, redemption) automatically leads one into the commitment of liberation from injustice, oppression, and poverty (that is, emancipation).

Distinguishing between and yet closely relating redemption and emancipation avoids the error of making the gospel either into a privatistic matter between God and the individual, or into a narrowly based message which focuses only on one form of bondage among many. To say this in another way, the gospel has to do with both attitudes and circumstances, with relationships and with actions, with being and with doing.

To me it appears to be true that some liberation theologians use socio-political liberation as the one and only hermeneutical or interpretive principle rather than as a theme among other themes. Thus, the Luke 4 narrative taken from Isaiah 61 is usually treated as a programmatic passage representing the whole New Testament instead of from the standpoint of Luke's particular concern for the poor and for women. Even in Luke this is only one theme among others. The almost exclusive concentration on a single theological theme is what James Gustafson has called "thematic unitarianism." We should not overlook the fact, however, that all interpreters function with a particular lens and from a particular point of view.

The selection of only one interpretive principle by liberation theologians has led some critics to say that liberation theology is possessed by a reductionist vision. This limited view, it is claimed, fails to regard Jesus as the one through whom God has acted to judge, redeem, and transform *all* of our transgression and injustices toward each other. If liberation theologies merely reduce the gospel to the contextual concerns of a particular ethnic or economic group, they can lose the sense of God's judging love in *all* dimensions of life and history because they have too narrowly defined the total meaning of bondage. As far as a general overview of liberation theologies is concerned, I share these critical questions with those who are raising them. Whether or not these claims can be sustained would depend on a careful analysis of a specific book or theological statement.

Few liberation theologians claim to be systematic in the traditional sense. Rather, they are holding before us that *particularistic theme* of God's action to liberate *from* certain forms of bondage and *for* a restored community. The faith question for us in dominant positions may not be whether liberation theology is wide enough in its selection of biblical images. The question is rather: if I were living under the conditions to which liberation theologians are addressing their message, would I be most interested in a comprehensive theological system or in the particularities of the biblical message and of Christian tradition which promise relief for human misery?

We should not demand the luxury of a universal context if it means theology must continually underemphasize the particularity of liberation from dehumanizing conditions and circumstances. If at times some liberation theologians seem to lump all issues together under the rubric of the rich and the poor, ethnic minorities and whites, or women and men, it might suggest the intensity of continual human anguish. Surely it is that fact which we need most of all to heed as Christians. What matters most deeply is that privileged and prosperous Christians hear that word that God is addressing to us through theologies of liberation.

Adequacy of Exodus as the Key Liberation Paradigm

As already mentioned, the Exodus event is by and large the number one example used by liberation theologies to substantiate their case for liberation today. A second criticism of liberation theology is that not only are the choices of liberation images too narrow to do justice to the biblical message, but also that the key example—Exodus—is used in a confused manner.

Among others John Howard Yoder has suggested that if Exodus were to be used as a model rather than as a mere slogan, it would suggest withdrawal rather than change within the existing society. The Israelites did not change Egypt by remaining in Egypt. They left Egypt.

> Exodus is not a paradigm for how all kinds of groups with all kinds of values can attain all kinds of salvation. . . . To transpose the motif of liberation out of that distinct historical framework and thereby also away from the distinct historical identity of the God of Abraham, Isaac, and Jacob, into some kind of general theistic affirmation of liberation, is to separate the biblical message from its foundation.[8]

Yoder goes on to say,

> Over against the paradigm of leaving Egypt and destroying Pharaoh on the way, we find in the Old Testament, more often, another model of how to live under a pagan oppressor. It is the way of Diaspora. This is the model taken over by the New Testament church and the model as well for two millennia of rabbinic Judaism. . . . The form of liberation in the biblical witness is not the guerilla campaign against an oppressor culminating in assassination and military defeat, but the creation of a confessing community which is viable without or against the force of the state.[9]

Yoder's point of view is informed by a steadfast commitment to nonviolent change. His reflections on Exodus as a model will be particularly challenging to those who advocate a liberation of violent revolution. To say the least he questions any simplistic transfer of the Exodus event to other historical situations, and he calls our attention to other biblical themes—exile, captivity, the cross, the giving of the law, and the scattering of the faithful. I believe that Yoder performs a favor for liberation theologians in calling for a deeper analysis of the form and meaning of liberation to match the language of liberation already in use.

I expect that Exodus is one event among several that can legitimately be employed in a theology of liberation, especially if one interprets liberation to involve both redemption and emancipation as suggested earlier. It may not be able to bear the weight unambiguously attributed to it by liberation theologies as a whole. At the same time it can be answered that the Exodus model focuses on God's action and purpose, not the historical specifics of Israel's movement.

Replacement of One Oppressor by Another

Some critics of liberation theology, on the basis of historical examples, believe that liberation theology merely seeks to exchange the positions of power and powerlessness in the world. While revolutionary change always incurs the risk of exchanging one ideological tyranny for another, the authors of liberation whom I've read are clear on this danger.

"We must love everyone, but it is not possible to love everyone in the same way. We love the oppressed by liberating them from their misery, and the oppressors by liberating them from their sin."[10] "All theologies of liberation, whether done in a black or a feminist or a Third World perspective, will be abortive of the liberation they seek unless they finally go beyond the apocalyptic, sectarian model of the oppressor and the oppressed. The oppressed must rise to a perspective that affirms a universal humanity as the ground of their own self-identity, and also to a power for self-criticism."[11]

The message of liberation theology is not a role reversal in which the dominant and the dominated exchange places (although Gutiérrez, with tongue in cheek, has suggested that such a reversal would at least be different and that taking turns might be fair!). It seems clear that liberation is for all, and therefore liberation theologies seek not a replacement, but the advent of styles, structures, and systems that bring an end to servitude and a new reality that recognizes the worth of all persons. What seems much less clear is the alternative view of power relations being proposed and the methods for bringing about a new system, especially in the United States. I'll comment on this further in the next section (utopian tendencies).

Liberation, seen by most Christian theologians to be inevitably connected with the kingdom of God and with the biblical concept of reconciliation, does not call for replacement by reversal of roles. It does call for the replacement of the values inherent in present powers and principalities. This call may sound like good news or like bad news, depending on where our identity and purpose for being are grounded. Of course, whether or not actual liberation movements follow the dictates of these Christian theologians is always an open question. Anyone familiar with history knows that the idealism of revolutions has frequently soured into ideologies as harsh and inhuman as those which were overturned. Today's champions of the poor may be tomorrow's defenders of the privileged and the powerful. Even so we cannot allow the well attested unpredictability of human nature to become an excuse for supporting exploitation and oppression.

Naiveté and Utopian Tendencies in Theologizing

Liberation theologies are sometimes criticized for their over-confidence in human possibilities. They call for radical changes in entrenched and powerful systems. They tend to see sin and salvation in corporate terms, and some critics wonder if they will repeat the mistakes of early twentieth-century liberal theology in identifying social change with the kingdom of God.

When you are not living in oppressed conditions, you can mistakenly conclude that theologies of liberation undervalue the possibilities of faith in the presence of severe limitations, or in the absence of political-economic justice. Is the human condition of oppression overemphasized and the human condition of finitude underemphasized? Even some who have experienced absence of political freedom have come to have confidence in a faith that struggles against tyranny, not because it will necessarily be successful or effective, but because that is the only way to become or remain a human being.

In the novel Bread and Wine the author, Ignazio Silone, struggles with this theme through the book's main figure, Pietro Spina, a revolutionary agent. At one point Spina declares, "You can live in a dictatorship and be free—on one condition: that you fight the dictatorship. The man who fights for what he thinks is right is free. But you can live in the most democratic country on earth and if you're lazy, obtuse, or servile within yourself, you're not free. Even without any violent coercion, you're a slave."[12]

While there can be inner freedom in the midst of violent coercion and slavery in the midst of political freedom, that is hardly a reason to disdain the imperative of changing systems that are producing poverty, greater disparity between the poor and the affluent, and the growing spectre of an earth exhausted of its resources. The kingdom of God has never become a fully realized fact, yet its promise and claim continue to be basic to the Christian interpretation of the gospel. If people are starving or living an utterly servile existence, especially with the blessing or benign neglect of the Christian church, they can hardly be blamed for expecting a concept of grace that calls for repentance from the powerful or that promises good news in the form of historical change. Those who are living their lives under the heel of someone else's boot are not likely to overestimate the possibilities of human goodness in this world! The main *intent* of liberation theologies as I hear them is not a utopian assumption about historical change; rather it is the assumption that commitment to Jesus Christ is to take seriously one's own involvement in the struggle for liberation.

While the intent of liberation theologies is not utopian, a question does remain as to the adequacy of their theories of power relations and social change. Of course one can point to revolution as an answer, an approach that may have genuine viability in some Third World countries in spite of the many dangers, both theologically and pragmatically. Or one can hope solely for God's liberating power to bring about historical change beyond our worldly wisdom and capacity to forecast or to formulate in theory. Even so, a liberation theology uninformed by an alternative theory of power relations may be more rhetoric than reality. In the United States, for example, how do liberation theologies confront the cultural and social coerciveness of our society?

The reflections of Tex Sample have been helpful to me in raising some hard questions along these lines.

> It seems to me that an end to oppression even in relative and broken ways requires a reversal of the fundamental direction that power realities are presently taking. That is, the emerging centralization of power in massive corporate complexes and its resultant systemic exploitation is the wave of the future as it presently looks. [13]

As I attempt to comprehend liberation theologies, I hear them bringing judgment on the present order and reminding us that it is a mistake to make evil systems the ultimate norm for what is either possible or desirable in history. These theologies do not dismiss the moral ambiguity that characterizes all social existence, nor do they call for a perfect social order. But in my judgment they do need to continue a great deal of hard homework in working through questions of alternative power systems and the methods by which these systems might come into being. The same imperative applies to privileged and prosperous Christians for the sake of our common emancipation.

Possessive Attitude Toward Christ and Divisive, Exclusive Ecclesiology

James Cone has written that Jesus is black. Vine Deloria pictures God as red. Feminist theologians have questioned the male pronoun for God. What astonishes me is not the fact of these assertions, but the way that some privileged and prosperous Christians react to them. The fact is that, historically speaking, God has functioned in our theology—and in our societal priorities—as a white, affluent male. The assertion that women have been excluded from shared power in the life of the church needs no supporting data. That Jesus Christ has been a "white Christ" is well attested when we look at the history of the dominant church in America and at the use of power. The time is long overdue to recognize that Jesus Christ is of all colors, races, and nations. Any decent theology of the Incarnation will insist that Jesus Christ, the Universal One, is identified in word and deed in a very particular way with the hungry, the thirsty, the naked, the homeless, and the forgotten people of the world.

We should not be surprised, then, when liberation theologians seem to make exclusive claims for the identification of the living Christ with their particular oppressed group. There is very little in the New Testament to support any claim of the privileged and the prosperous that Jesus Christ is at home in our comfort, our ease, and our lukewarm, convenient religion. Indeed, with the exception of Joseph of Arimathea, the only specific instance in any of the gospels where an affluent individual is depicted in a favorable manner is the story of Zacchaeus in Luke 19. And this was a result of a major transformation on the part of Zacchaeus in response to Jesus, a radical change in both attitude and act toward the poor!

The criticisms of liberation theology that have been assessed have had mostly to do with theological perspectives. Some of these critical assessments have genuine substance, and I believe that liberation theology will do well to give consideration to them. Nevertheless, we will be playing ecclesiastical games if we allow theological disputes to diminish the claims of the poor and the disinherited of the earth for a decent and dignified life.

For me the more serious arena of struggle is that of personal faith and decision. As Robert McAfee Brown puts it, "Liberation theology tells us that we are on the wrong side and that if we do not change sides, things will be very rough for us in the future. But we immediately realize that if we do change sides, things will be very rough for us in the present."[14] This is the decision with which we must struggle.

Notes

Chapter One:
Out of Oppression and into Restored Community

1. As I look back now in the light of my present theological posture, I would not automatically assume a building project for a new congregation.

2. James H. Cone, *God of the Oppressed* (New York: Seabury Press, 1975).

3. Gustavo Gutiérrez, *A Theology of Liberation* (Maryknoll, New York: Orbis Books, 1973), p. 10.

4. I use this trilogy to suggest the major theological movements of liberation. I am aware that one person might be aptly described by more than one of these labels.

5. *The Kansas City Times,* editorial, October 2, 1976. All of the figures in the paragraph are from this source.

6. Rosemary R. Ruether, *New Woman-New Earth* (New York: Seabury Press, 1975).

7. Linda Phelps, "Women's Rights and Women's Liberation: Social and Cultural Revolution," mimeographed paper.

8. E. F. Schumacher, *Small is Beautiful* (New York: Harper and Row, 1975), especially Chapter One, "The Problem of Production," pp. 13-22.

9. José Miguez Bonino, *Doing Theology in a Revolutionary Situation* (Philadelphia: Fortress Press, 1975), pp. 14-15. For a penetrating and persuasive discussion of North American dominance of Latin America, I recommend Chapter Two, "Understanding Our World." The United States economic occupation of Latin American countries, enforced by political and military power, is in my judgment clearly documented.

10. For a description of these transformations read Chapter Three, "The Awakening of the Christian Conscience," in Miguez Bonino's *Doing Theology in a Revolutionary Situation.*

11. Valerie Russell, "Racism and Sexism: A Collective Struggle," 1972, mimeographed paper.

12. Ruether, *New Woman-New Earth,* p. 132.

13. Gutiérrez, *A Theology of Liberation,* pp. 158-159.

14. Letty Russell, *Human Liberation in a Feminist Perspective—A Theology* (Philadelphia: Westminster Press, 1971), p. 110.

15. J. Deotis Roberts, *Liberation and Reconciliation: A Black Theology* (Philadelphia: Westminster Press, 1971), p. 29.

16. Russell, *Human Liberation in a Feminist Perspective.* It should be noted,

however, that a great deal of previous theologizing has proceeded inductively from experience: to an extent at least, Luther, Wesley, Schleiermacher, Reinhold Neibuhr, and Rauschenbusch.

17. Ibid., p. 54.

18. Gutiérrez, *A Theology of Liberation,* p. 232.

19. Russell, *Human Liberation in a Feminist Perspective,* pp. 91-92.

Chapter Two:
The Anatomy of Liberation: The Foolishness of God

1. Conrad Hyers, "The Nativity as Divine Comedy," *The Christian Century,* December 11, 1974, pp. 1168-1172.

2. John C. Bennett, *The Radical Imperative* (Philadelphia: Westminster Press, 1975), p. 14.

Chapter Three:
The Blessed Disturbance in the Blessed Assurance

1. James H. Cone, *A Black Theology of Liberation* (Philadelphia: Lippincott, 1970), pp. 185-186.

2. I acknowledge indebtedness at this point to Robert McAfee Brown for his thoughts in *Is Faith Obsolete?* (Philadelphia: Westminster Press, 1974), Chapter Five, especially pages 120-140.

3. Ibid., p. 126.

4. Ibid., p. 127.

5. Rosemary Ruether, *Liberation Theology* (New York: Paulist Press, 1972), p. 171.

Chapter Four:
The Good Life Redefined: Abrahamic/Zacchaean Lifestyles

1. *Newsweek,* August 15, 1977: "Let's Bring Back Heroes," an article by William J. Bennett.

2. Charles Schulz, *Peanuts,* syndicated cartoon.

3. Mary I. Buckley, "Freedom as Personal and Public Liberation," in *Liberation, Revolution, and Freedom,* edited by Thomas M. McFadden (New York: Seabury Press, 1975), p. 35.

4. Dietrich Bonhoeffer, *Letters and Papers from Prison,* edited by Eberhard Bethge (New York: Macmillan Co., 1971), quoted and paraphrased from p. 361.

5. Helder Camara, *The Desert Is Fertile* (Maryknoll, N.Y.: Orbis Books, 1974).

6. Ibid., p. 15.

7. Robert McAfee Brown, *Is Faith Obsolete?,* p. 139.

8. Abraham Heschel, *The Wisdom of Heschel,* selected by Ruth Marcus

Goodhill (New York: Farrar, Straus, and Giroux, 1975), p. 40.

9. A June 8-15, 1977, article in *The Christian Century,* "Sharing the Wealth: The Church as Biblical Model for Public Policy," by Ronald J. Sider, was helpful in shaping a broad biblical overview of economics.

10. Ibid., p. 564.

11. Albert Schweitzer, *The Quest of the Historical Jesus* (New York: Macmillan Company, 1968), p. 403.

12. This paragraph is adapted from my article in *The Center Letter,* Center for Parish Development, vol. 6, no. 3, March 1976.

13. The material on male mystiques and the new male humanness is adapted and amended from my article in *Christian Advocate,* vol. 16, no. 13, July 6, 1972, pp. 7-8.

Chapter Five:
Nurturing Life Systems with People Priorities

1. Robert Heilbroner, *An Inquiry into the Human Prospect* (New York: Norton, 1974).

2. *The Christian Century,* July 9-16, 1975, p. 663.

3. E. F. Schumacher, *Small Is Beautiful* (New York: Harper & Row, 1973), pp. 40-41.

4. Ibid., p. 14.

5. Ibid., p. 15.

6. Theodore Roszak, Introduction to *Small is Beautiful,* p. 9.

7. Schumacher, *Small Is Beautiful,* pp. 204-205.

8. Charles Baughman, "World Hunger from the Biblical Perspective" (Kansas City, Mo.: Saint Paul School of Theology, 1977).

9. Quoted by Schumacher, *Small Is Beautiful,* p. 33.

10. Friends Committee on National Legislation, testimony by Edward F. Snyder on behalf of the Friends Committee on National Legislation before the House Budget Committee on the Fiscal 1977 Budget, February 2, 1976.

11. An increasing number of publications within the economic and professional community are raising the question of alternative systems. In addition to E. F. Schumacher's *Small Is Beautiful,* two recent examples among many are *Business Civilization in Decline,* by Robert Heilbroner (New York: Norton, 1976) and *Toward a Human World Order,* by Gerald and Patricia Mische (New York: Paulist Press, 1977).

Chapter Six:
Improvisations on Liberation and Evangelism

1. For example the writings of Frank E. X. Dance, Susanne K. Langer, and Walter J. Ong, S.J.

2. Obtained from the keynote address of Dr. George G. Hunter, III, to the United Methodist Council on Evangelism, Des Moines, Iowa, January 11, 1977.

3. Reuel L. Howe, *The Miracle of Dialogue* (New York: Seabury Press, 1964), p. 149.

4. Albert C. Outler, *Evangelism in the Wesleyan Spirit* (Nashville: Tidings, 1971), p. 56.

5. George G. Hunter, III, ed., *Rethinking Evangelism* (Nashville: Tidings, 1971), especially pp. 52-55.

6. From an address given at Drew University, as reported by Religious News Service, *The United Methodist Reporter*.

7. Helmut Gollwitzer, *The Rich Christians and Poor Lazarus* (New York: Macmillan Co., 1970), p. 1. Gollwitzer's figures may not be entirely correct, but this should not erode the truth of his assertion.

8. Outler, *Evangelism in the Wesleyan Spirit*, p. 32.

9. That statement may be an approximation of an original saying by E. Stanley Jones.

10. Victor Paul Furnish, *The Love Command in the New Testament* (Nashville: Abingdon Press, 1972), p. 213.

11. John C. Bennett, *The Radical Imperative* (Philadelphia: Westminster Press, 1975), pp. 49-50.

Chapter Seven:
Liberation Liturgy as the Work of The People

1. H. Grady Hardin, Joseph D. Quillian, Jr., and James F. White, *The Celebration of the Gospel* (Nashville: Abingdon, 1964), p. 33.

2. Paul W. Hoon, *The Integrity of Worship* (Nashville: Abingdon, 1971), p. 294.

3. Adapted from my article, "Worship Transcends Language," published in the *United Methodist Reporter*, December 31, 1976.

4. James F. White, *Christian Worship in Transition* (Nashville: Abingdon, 1976), p. 136.

5. For insights into and aids for lay involvement in worship, see Wilfred M. Bailey, *Awakened Worship* (Nashville: Abingdon, 1972), especially Part III.

6. Hoon, *Integrity of Worship*, p. 338.

7. The term "non-eucharistic" is used only as a contrasting term, since all Christian worship is of course eucharistic or based on thanksgiving.

8. Dom Gregory Dix, *The Shape of the Liturgy* (London: Dacre Press, 1945).

9. John A. T. Robinson, *Liturgy Coming to Life* (Philadelphia: Westminster Press, 1960), p. 19.

10. Ibid.

11. For example, Joseph W. Mathews, "Common Worship in the Life of the Church," mimeographed article.

12. *The Methodist Hymnal* (1939), #214. The writer of the text is anonymous.

13. Hoon, *Integrity of Worship*, pp. 17 and 31-32.

14. Ibid., p. 54.

15. This does not suggest a conflict between corporate worship and individual or personal devotions. As a matter of fact a strong case can be made for the indispensable connection of the two.

16. Robinson, *Liturgy Coming to Life*, p. 31.

17. J. G. Davies, *Worship and Mission* (New York: Associated Press, 1967), p. 151. The edition to which Davies refers is the 1928 edition, not the current one.

18. William K. McElvaney, "Is Our Communion Liturgy Christian?" *Christian Advocate*, September 23, 1965, pp. 9-10.

19. Massey Shepherd, Jr., *Liturgy and Education* (New York: The Seabury Press, 1965), p. 110.

20. Rosemary R. Ruether, *New Woman-New Earth*, p. xiii.

21. Letty M. Russell, ed., *The Liberating Word (A Guide to Nonsexist Language)* (Philadelphia: The Westminster Press, 1976).

22. Herman Schmidt and David Power, eds., *Politics and Liturgy*, Concilium 92 (New York: Herder and Herder, 1974), p. 9.

23. Ibid., pp. 29-30.

Appendix:
Soundings on Theologies of the Oppressed

1. William K. McElvaney, *Christ's Suburban Body* (Nashville: Abingdon Press, 1970), p. 57.

2. Cone, *God of the Oppressed*, p. 137.

3. John Dominic Crossan, *In Parables* (New York: Harper and Row, 1973), p. 23.

4. Gunther Bornkamm, *Jesus of Nazareth* (New York: Harper and Brothers, 1960), p. 64.

5. Robert A. Spivey and D. Moody Smith, Jr., *Anatomy of the New Testament* (New York: Macmillan Co., 1969), pp. 190-191.

6. Rudolf Bultmann, *Theology of the New Testament* (New York: C. Scribner's Sons, 1951), vol. I, p. 4.

7. Schubert M. Ogden, *Faith and Freedom: Toward a Theology of Liberation*, from Laity Week Lectures delivered at Perkins School of Theology, February 10-12, 1977, p. 9. A slightly different wording has been used in the published form of this material in Schubert M. Ogden, *Faith and Freedom* (Nashville: Abingdon, 1979), p. 36.

8. John Howard Yoder, "Probing the Meaning of Liberation," *Sojourners*, September 1976, pp. 26-29.

9. Ibid., p. 29.

10. Gutiérrez, *A Theology of Liberation*, quoting Giulio Girardi, p. 285.

11. Rosemary Ruether, *Liberation Theology* (New York: Paulist Press, 1972), p. 16.

12. Ignazio Silone, *Bread and Wine* (New York: New American Library, 1937, 1962), p. 283.

13. From conversations with Tex Sample, Professor of Church and Society, Saint Paul School of Theology, Kansas City, Missouri.

14. Robert McAfee Brown, *Is Faith Obsolete?* (Philadelphia: Westminster Press, 1974), p. 124.